Praise for

As the top-performing ng community, I can't think of a better person to write a book about having a positive mindset and staying focused to reach a goal than Melissa Corsiatto.

With a type A personality and a go-getter attitude, I've witnessed her out-work her peers time and time again.

She struggled with Addiction as long as she did and then completely turned her life around to create financial freedom for her family. She's proof of what goal setting is, working hard, and having a positive mindset can and will create the life you dream of living.

I highly recommend you dive into the pages of Darkness Through Addiction and gather all the diamonds of info waiting for you in its pages, especially if you're someone that struggles with negative self-talk and wants a process for finding light in your darkness.

Darkness Through Addiction is the book for you.

Cari Higham
Multiple 7-Figure Earner & Bestselling Author of
You Got This Girl: Overcoming Obstacles, Smashing Goals & Creating an Abundant Life

Life is indeed full of challenges - at the best of times - I can't imagine the struggles and things that have to overcome when faced with addiction.

Melissa has overcome her struggle with addiction in ways that have resulted in her becoming more than most would ever dream of achieving.

Since I met Melissa, I have come to know her "heart" and her "determination" to continue to improve her own life as well as the lives of others!

She shows her passion and focuses on discovering ways to be of service to others since having overcome one of the biggest challenges many faces in today's world – addiction.

I have great admiration and appreciation for you, Melissa. You continue to show up each day with continued strength and passion for positively changing people's lives! Thank you for being you!

Angela Domet

Sales Coach

We are very proud of Melissa. She went through a lot, but it turned out good in the end. Melissa came out a stronger person after going through what she did. But if it wasn't for her Mom's strength, I don't know what she would be doing now. Melissa needed her and her family.

-Uncle Dale

When I met Melissa, we instantly connected. She told me this heart-wrenching story of how she overcame this addiction. I immediately wanted to talk to her about writing a book about it.

The first time we spoke about the book, there were many tears and many fears; however, over the last few months, watching her blossom into this powerful human who is about to change lives is why I do what I do.

You will be touched by the perseverance she had to live and overcome something most of us would've given up on life for. I am So very proud of you, girl! And I am honored to be your coach through it all.

Tina Torres,
The Gratitude Specialist
Founder of 120 days to Best Seller

I met Melissa well over 20 years ago. We both were not focused on our health or wellness back then but fast forward 20 years, and my dear friend is a true leader and inspiration for many.

Not only has she beat all her addictions, but she is also a massive leader in the health and wellness industry & is constantly helping other people/ moms/ women strive to be the best person they can be. I am proud to call Melissa my friend and look up to her in many ways. Starting from the bottom and working your way up takes so much determination and effort!

Melissa Corsiatto has so much input and value to share, as she has been there & done that! Keep up the incredible work, Melissa! Your motivation to your family, kids, and friends is outstanding, and you are a true leader. Once you put your mind to something, there is no stopping you!

Alexa Herbert
Network Marker

I have been amazed by Melissa since the day I met her. She has a zest for life that I don't see in many people. She goes for it when she wants something, and there is no stopping her. I am excited about all the lives she will impact with this book. I have known and worked with her for many years. When Melissa shared her journey through addiction, how she overcame it and had been clean for 13 years, I was blown away. For someone to come back from so close to death takes nothing short of a miracle.

Brandy Shaver
7 Figure, Coach

Melissa is a force. Whatever she sets her mind to, consider it done. She has a rare determination, such a high standard of perseverance, integrity, and honesty that is inspirational. It's a privilege and honor to be working as a coach alongside her. She has experienced dark nights of the soul, which is why she can shine so brightly now. Her level of focus and commitment is matched by her intelligence and caring. Melissa's story is one of courage and triumph that we can all take lessons from.

Alex Sessa
6 Figure Sales Coach

When I first met Melissa Corsiatto, I was immediately struck by her high energy and will to win. Little did I know about the journey she had been through and the trials and tribulations she had faced in her life.

What Melissa has accomplished in her life is nothing short of remarkable. She joined my sales academy and very quickly secured a place on one of my coaching teams, becoming the top coach on that team within a couple of months and holding that position ever since.

The energy and enthusiasm she brings to her position as a coach are incredible. Her willingness to learn and grow as a coach and person are exceptionally inspiring. She does not accept second best and is constantly finding ways to improve and excel in everything she does.

It has been an enormous pleasure for me to play a small part in her journey; I am honored to see her change and impact so many of her clients' lives along the way through her coaching.

Her positive attitude and incredible mindset will undoubtedly impact anyone who comes into contact with Melissa that she imparts on people.

Fraser Thom
7 Figure Coaching Mentor

I met Debbie when she came to work on the same unit as me. She was a valued co-worker with a strong work ethic, and we soon became friends and confidantes. I worried about her well-being as she shared certain situations in her private life with me. It became evident very quickly that Debbie was the glue that held her family together and that she would do whatever she could to provide the support needed. Her unconditional love for her family, strength, and positivity in the face of adversity was highly inspirational to me.

Initially, I knew of Melissa only in the context of hearing about choices she made that affected her health, well-being, and safety. With guidance, support, and unconditional love from Debbie, Melissa forged a path of recovery that would see her make incredibly positive changes in her life.

Melissa has become a trusted entrepreneur who assists others in becoming the best they can be. She focuses on her health as well as that of her family. The health and happiness of her family, making beautiful memories with them, and giving them unconditional love, as Debbie gave to her, are the cornerstones of Melissa's life today.

-Donna Reid
Friend

Melissa's book is a must-read, whether you're going through difficult times or not.

This woman is an incredible coach and mentor, helping students get crystal clear on where they want to be and understand what's keeping them stuck.

She is one of the most focused and determined people I know. When she sets a goal, nothing stops her from getting it done and excelling at whatever she does.

But it wasn't always this way for Melissa.

She will take you on her journey of 16 years of drug addiction, and no matter what you're going through right now, you'll have the tools and the inspiration to get through it and turn your life around.

Congratulations, Melissa, for having the courage to tell your story. I'm so proud of you!!

Fran Loubser
Beach Boss Influencer, Coach, and Mentor

When I first met Melissa, I was struck by her professionalism, commitment to service, and willingness to support and mentor all those who cross her path. After getting to know her a little better, it became evident that she is a dedicated and loving wife, mother, daughter, sister, and friend. Her warmth and steadiness of character, her drive for success, and her passion for life –are qualities that drew me to her and made her stand out as someone I wanted to know better. In her company is to be heard, uplifted, and understood.

In those early days of becoming friends, I could never have guessed the dark challenges that Melissa has faced, nor the grit and determination she had needed to not only overcome those challenges but to triumph over them.

Now, as she shares this journey with readers, her persistent self-awareness and vulnerability open the door for others who share similar struggles to walk through, come alive, and flourish as she has. Melissa writes as an actual act of service – as a signpost for those unsure of their life's direction.

Lisa Dunlop-Clark
Sales Coach

I first got to know Melissa through our trainer/ client relationship at the gym. From our first session together, I knew something uniquely special about her as she put her heart and soul into each rep of every set of every workout. A few months into our training, when Melissa was getting deeper into her contest prep, she confided in me about her past life experiences and her struggles with addictions. I was blown away by how honest, open, and authentic she was and continues to be as she strives daily to live her best life as a wife, Mom, boss lady, and gym badass.

Melissa truly epitomizes the idea that "energy and persistence conquer all things," and I could not be prouder of this fantastically energetic, brave, authentic, and inspirational human being I am lucky enough to call a friend.

Jason Petrie
Personal Trainer

The Darkness Through Addiction

A mother and daughter's heart-wrenching story

Melissa Corsiatto
Deborah Hamm

Copyright © 2022 by Melissa Corsiatto & Deborah Hamm. **The Darkness Through Addiction. A mother and daughter's heart-wrenching story.** All Rights Reserved.

No part of this publication may be reproduced, distributed, or transmitted by any form or by any means, including photocopying, recording, or any other electronic or mechanical methods, without prior written permission by the publisher, except in the case of brief quotations embodied in critical reviews and certain other non-commercial uses permitted by copyright law.

Unless otherwise indicated, all scriptures are taken from the New International Version (NIV)

This book is a memoir. It reflects the author's present recollections of experiences over time. Some names and characteristics have been changed, some events have been compressed, and some dialogue has been recreated.

Melissa Corsiatto
Deborah Hamm

Alberta, Canada

Instagram: @melissacorsiatto
Facebook: www.facebook.com/melissa.hamm.98
Website: www.MelissaCorsiatto.com

For speaking inquiries, permission requests, and bulk order purchase options, contact: mhamm502@gmail.com

ISBN: 9798799185176

Dedication

This book is dedicated to my grandma and grandpa up in heaven, to my husband and two boys.

Table of Contents

Foreword	i
Introduction	iii
Chapter One: A Nightmare in a child's eyes	1
Chapter Two: A Mom's Perspective: A New Beginning	13
Chapter Three: Just When You Think Everything Was going right	23
Chapter Four: The Nightmare Begins	37
Chapter Five: Handcuffs and shackles	41
Chapter Six: This is, really, a Nightmare	51
Chapter Seven: I looked death in the eye - the deepest of my addiction	59
Chapter Eight: The valley of death	65
Chapter Nine: The Death Bed	73
Chapter Ten: The Change	79
Chapter 11 My Next Chapter In Life: "You're always one decision away from a totally different life."	83
Chapter 12 My letter to you	95
Acknowledgments	109
About The Authors	111

Foreword

I can't think of a better person to write a book about finding Darkness Through Addiction than Melissa Corsiatto.

It has been a blessing to listen to her story and what she has had to overcome to create the life of freedom she has for her family.

I've watched as she has had to overcome every obstacle thrown her way from physical & financial stress to negative self-talk, all while striving to be the best person she can be and stay sober.

I first met her through one of my business partners and immediately recognized something special about her.

I could tell she had a positive attitude and a magnetic personality that anyone would want to work with.

Her go-getter attitude and type A personality made her stand out.

She was hungry for success and knew she had what it took to finally take her business to the next level if she could only tap into the right strategies.

She was determined to change her circumstances, and I watched as she out-worked everyone around her to make success happen.

She's the top coach in the private coaching community she serves, is growing a successful team inside the network marketing industry and has created a life that most people dream of living.

You'll learn about Melissa because she puts her best step forward into everything she does. When she decides she's going to make things happen, she manifests it into existence by hard work, determination, and true grit.

I've personally watched her grow her income, business, and brand over the past few years, and more important than that, she's able to help her students and teammates get results as well.

If you want to know what it takes to overcome addiction, be successful and faster, take your life to the next level. Then I highly recommend you read Darkness Through Addiction right away and implement every single concept Melissa shares.

Your business and life will be better off because of it.

Melissa, my friend, I'm so freaking proud of you!

It has been an honor to watch and help you grow into the badass leader, coach, and trainer you are.

All who know you are blessed to learn from you, and I'm forever grateful for our friendship and partnership.

With love,

Whit Higham

7-Figure Entrepreneur

Introduction

No, it's not a coincidence you are here for a reason.

Something drew you to this book, and my Mom and I are so excited you're here. We will share our deep dark journey through the eyes of an addict and a parent who experienced her daughter at her darkest moments in life.

Releasing this book has not been an easy task for us to complete. We had to relive hard times that we have always wanted to forget and put in the past.

But it's through us going into these darkest times during our lives to share with you the journey that we pray to help someone out there suffering in their own life.

This book will help you understand (through the lens of my eyes and my Mom's eyes) the thoughts, the feelings, the emotions, and the fear of both sides.

As a child, I dreamed of a fairytale life. You know, living that perfect life. Growing up having a happy family, everyone's getting along, doing fun things as a family. A life where everyone is always laughing and having a good time, and when I grow up, go off to college, get a good job, find a man of my dreams, have kids—and have that everlasting happy life.

That dream shattered when my parents split up at age 9, ripping my heart and dreams apart. Everything broke right before my eyes.

As I moved into my teenage life, I began to rebel and become the child from hell.

Struggling with abandonment issues and not having my Dad around, I began to seek out older men, leading to alcohol and drugs.

The journey I went through for the next 16 years was far from sunshine and rainbows. My life turned upside down, losing not only everything around me, but I also lost my family and lost myself during this journey. I was well on my way to death.

If you're the addict reading this, please know that you're not alone and never have to be alone. There is help out there for you. I know it's dark, I know it's hard, I know it's lonely, and I know that sometimes you feel like giving up and going deeper into that addiction, but no matter where you are in your journey, please know that you can overcome anything you are facing, you got this! If I can do it, you can do it too.

The chapters ahead were hard to write as it took me back to the darkest days in my life, days I wanted never to remember again, but I knew – within my heart – it was the right thing I needed to do. Not just for me but because of YOU.

If you're the parent, please know, this was a challenging book for me to write. We would never like to see our children hurting or going through addiction. Reliving those dark days was horrifying. There were some dark days. But as we were writing about it and remembering what had happened in our lives has helped us heal. I had never heard or seen how Melissa felt about things until reading her story. This process allowed me to know the feelings that she kept inside. It also let Melissa know the things she didn't know about me. That is why it was healing.

Today, I am thankful that the days that I thought would never have an end are finally over.

As I wrote this book and contemplated our humanity, some people might say children are resilient, but are they? I left their Dad, and the house we lived in for a better life. Although not all things were terrible and we had some good times, things didn't go as planned. I would never have imagined what lay ahead.

As you read through these pages, know that I wrote as a mom with the conviction that you find hope, despite why this book caught your eye, if you could be the addict or the broken parent of the addict. I hope our story gives you the strength to endure wherever your addict's journey is. I hope you can see that with faith that you get through this.

I have faith in a Higher power which to me is God. Without that faith, I probably would not have gotten through a lot of this journey. The fact that my parents were always my cheering section. I could call them anytime to cry or talk and get their advice. You must have those in your journey. And most important of all, remember "someone has to believe in them." And when they are sick and tired of being sick and tired, THEY will do something about it.

After reading this book, you may think differently. I know I did. Children become adults shaped by their own experiences.

The following pages will be hard to read, but I want you to know that you got this no matter what stage you're at as the addict or as the parent/spouse/loved one. Know that there is so much more to life.

Chapter One
A Nightmare in A Child's Eyes

I never thought I would be that girl everyone called a drug addict.

I was the type of girl who lived a fairytale life when I was little—having a family of 2 older brothers and one younger sister, and two parents who seemed to be that happily ever after couple.

My parents were pig farmers as well as they also raised cattle and chickens. We lived in a beautiful log house, with a big picture window in the living room decorated with orange lacy curtains. The window was facing south into the massive garden in the yard surrounded by trees, and in the distance, you could see our crops in the field, a wood-burning fireplace where we gathered around as a family on those cold winter nights. Having a few bedrooms upstairs where my sister and I shared a room, my brother's bedroom was beside us with Mom and Dad in the master across the hall. My oldest brother had his room in the basement.

The basement is where we kids spent time if we were not outside playing. Lots of room to play, have fun, and just be kids. The porch, which was an addition to the home, was the entryway into the house. I remember it smelt like pigs' shit, haha, that smell I will never forget. But it was only there once you entered the house; it always smelt like home-cooked meals.

We lived the life of a farm family.

THE DARKNESS THROUGH ADDICTION

I remember all the fantastic times my siblings and I played outside building forts, playing with trucks, making forts in the bales, playing war, yes, just running around freely, laughing, and having such a great time. Having two older brothers, I was a tomboy growing up.

When my younger sister was born, I was in love. I was like a little girl who pretended she had a baby. I took care of her, I read to her, I cuddled her. I was the best big sister ever.

Every evening my Mom would have a home-cooked meal on the table, and we all came together to share our day.

During the harvest seasons, I would go with my Dad in the tractor, and man being that tomboy I was, it sure felt good to be by my Dad's side doing "boy" stuff. As my Dad drove the tractor, I would sit there in my glory, smiling ear to ear. If I was not with my Dad in that tractor, I was jumping in the vehicle any chance I could get when my Mom would take the meals out to the men in the field.

During the winter months, Dad would take us out Skidooing to clear our minds. I remember us as kids sitting on this oversized truck hood as Dad would pull us around the yard. Our older Skidoo gave off the smell of a two-stroke exhaust, and I loved that smell.

One year my Dad decided to build us a treehouse. I think we bugged him enough to give in – LOL – finally. This treehouse was the coolest thing ever, having stairs up to the house, emerged through a hole, walls all around with that roof that made it complete. My siblings and I spend lots of time there.

One year we got a ton of snow, like I mean a ton. We were in our glory and spent most days outside playing and having fun. There was a huge drift in the pasture where the pigs were, and my Dad carved out holes and tunnels. It was the best fort ever. I remember playing in this snow fort for hours each day.

A NIGHTMARE IN A CHILD'S EYES

I even helped at odd times with chores in the pig barn and milking the cows, always wanting to be wherever my Dad was doing the things he was doing. It made me feel secure, and as the top boy, I was at heart. I was definitely "Daddy's little girl."

For the most part, from what I remember, my parents had a good relationship, but I know some fights happened due to alcohol. I know Dad consumed alcohol and got drunk, and that's when the arguments happened.

I remember being in my room sleeping and waking up to hear my parents arguing. Being so young, I didn't know what was happening, but I knew I was scared. I didn't know how to stop it. I wanted to make it stop, but I was so afraid to even come out of the room because I didn't want them to know I was hearing them. As the voices got louder, I became more scared and afraid they would come into my room and see that I was awake, so I hid in the closet, covering my ears, trying not to hear anything. So scared, not wanting to leave the room but knowing I had to because I had to pee so bad, I peed my pants and, sat in my room terrified even to come out.

These episodes began to happen more frequently, Dad began to drink more, and my parents seemed to argue more than they did before.

One day when my life came to a crashing halt, Mom sat me down and told me the devastating news, "we are moving into town because I am leaving your dad" gulp. As a little girl and one who was a daddy's little girl, it ripped my heart apart. I felt like my life was coming to an end.

I always looked forward to the weekends because I knew it meant time with my Dad. I would go to the farm, and he would cook me my favorite meals, sausages, Pierogies, or kraft dinner with buttermilk.

As a little girl, I would go to my dad's home on the weekends to spend a few nights with him, I remember going back to moms place on Sundays, and I would not shower or wash my clothes for a few days because I wanted to keep the scent of my Dad around me. I needed something that reminded me of him and I could feel he was with me even though I was not with him physically. It was a comforting thing for me, I guess.

So many emotions I had as a little girl after my parents split up. As a little girl, I remember thinking, why am I going through this, why don't my parents love each other, why did my parents split up, and why can't my parents just be together so we can live that happy life.

I was pissed at my Mom for leaving my Dad. She tore our family apart and ruined my life; why would she do that to me?

I still loved my Mom but could not understand why she wanted to hurt me. I was a broken little girl, who's life was shattered. I was sad for my Dad because I knew he was unhappy, lonely, and in a dark place, and there was nothing I could do about it.

On the Fridays I was going to stay with my Dad, my heart was complete, I was excited and so happy, I was that little girl jumping up and down and grinning ear to ear. But behind that happiness was a hurt little girl. I still was lonely, sad, and hurt.

Leaving Dad to go back to Mom's, was the hardest thing to do each week. Every week, I got heartbroken because I knew he would be alone, with nobody around him to comfort him during this difficult time. When he dropped me off, the sadness in his face and the tears in his eyes just tore me apart.

Our weekends looked like having fun, playing around, and wrestling around in the living room. I felt loved and happy when I was with my Dad. I knew he was also delighted, which made this little girl's day.

Then the day came that completely changed my life forever. Mom decided to move us to another province. She had a place for us, and she had landed an excellent job to start a life and create a future for us. Well, that's not what I thought; in my eyes, as a 12-year-old, I felt she was trying to take me away from my Dad and destroy my life even more. I was hurt, upset, and hated my Mom.

Looking back, she was doing the best for us but at that time, what was going through my mind was, you're doing this to rip me and take me away from my Dad. I was sad and very pissed at my Mom for her doing this. Why would she do this to me? I thought she was my Mom and loved me.

To this day, (this day is always in the back of my head). My heart was shattered. I felt like my whole life was taken away from me. As I gave my Dad a hug and a big kiss, not knowing when I would see him again, the tears began to flow down my face. Mom loaded us up in the vehicle. I remember looking back and waving to my Dad while blowing him hundreds of kisses as the tears continued to run down my face – and by this time, it was a waterfall. I still have the image of my Dad standing there looking like everything was taken away with sadness in his eyes. His jaw quivered; his shoulders lowered as if his life was taken away. For me, it was like my life was over—everything was taken away from me at once. I felt bad for my Dad, and I couldn't shake that sense of being lost as I watched my Dad get smaller in the distance.

I hated life, hated everything about it. It was terrible.

Coming from a small town and arriving at our new destination, I remember driving down Main Street, seeing the buildings, and thinking we were moving to a big city, LOL

Nervous and scared, I entered grade 7. As this 12-year-old girl who didn't think she would ever fit in or make any new friends.

Shortly into 7th grade, I met some other girls my age and was in class with, let's call them, Sally, Jessica, and Nancy.

They were already a pact, and they let me into their circle. I fit right in, and it felt great. As the year went on, we bonded and became best friends. We had some fun times together, sleepovers, hangouts after school. You know the song girls just want to have fun, well that was us all the time.

A few of my friends in the pact were into sports, particularly volleyball, which I liked and tried out for the junior team and made it.

But there was still something missing, always going to my friend's place, and most of them had a mom and Dad that were together. Knowing I lacked that in my life, I was jealous and missed my Dad.

I was not seeing my Dad that often because we lived so far away from each other was hard on me. We did have calls from him every Sunday, which I always looked forward to, but it was not the same.

Mom was always working. She worked a shift work schedule, which meant we didn't see her the days she was sleeping all day.

I was missing my Dad. I was also missing my Mom as she was always working.

As a 12-year-old girl, all I needed was a dad, I needed to be noticed and loved by a male figure, and I was missing that.

"One decision or choice you make can change your life and your family's life forever," and that's what it did for me.

As an innocent little girl looking for attention and acceptance, her dreams came true.

On a fall afternoon, walking home from school, my friends and I kept seeing this older fixed-up Chevy truck driving with two older "men" inside. Putting their attention on us every time they went by, peeking our interests each time. One time they decided to stop and chat with us. OMG, I was excited and nervous at the same time. I had butterflies in my belly, my palms were sweating, and I didn't know what to say. But inside, I feel so good and cool.

A NIGHTMARE IN A CHILD'S EYES

As curious little girls, we all giggled and walked up to the truck. These two men introduced themselves, let's call them "John" and "Jack," and asked us our names and how we were. I remember each man had a bottle of extra old stock beer in each hand. We chatted for a bit, and then they drove off.

The next day the same truck with the same guys was driving around, again curious but now really excited when they stopped to chat, this time they invited us into cruise around town. And, of course, we did. Asked us if we wanted a beer, and heck yes, we tried to fit in. These "men" were hot, and all I wanted to do was impress them.

They invited us over to a house party that would take place on the weekend. Of course, Mom would not let me attend. I wanted to go so badly. So, I got resourceful and developed a plan. I would have my friend, let's call her "Sue," come over for a sleepover, and we would pitch a tent in the backyard, then we could sneak out without my Mom knowing.

It was a plan, and this plan worked very well. We were able to make it to the party.

Getting there felt a bit out of place as we were the youngest ones there. We began to drink some beers. Feeling a bit intoxicated and more as I fitted in and relaxed, I remember John was all over me, kissing me, paying attention to me, making me feel loved. We ventured downstairs to a room. Well, you can only imagine what happened next.

I remember this time so vividly, nervous, scared, and unsure what to expect but just going with the flow. At that moment, I felt loved, something that I had been lacking for a while. It felt amazing to feel this way. My heart was warm, fluffy, and overflowing with joy, thinking, OMG, he loves me.

At 12, not knowing I should not have sex, here I was having a sexual relationship with a "man."

THE DARKNESS THROUGH ADDICTION

I wanted to be loved so much, held so badly, and I was willing to do anything to have it, even if this meant something so scary as losing my virginity at 12, even if it meant keeping it a secret.

Leaving the party, I was on top of the world, feeling loved and accepted by this man.

As a 12-year-old girl not having my Dad around, all I wanted was acceptance and love from a man, and that's what he was giving me.

As the weeks went on, John and Jake continued to pick me up after school, and we would cruise around town and have a beer or two. Spending this much time with John, I began to fall in love with him, and I thought he was falling in love with me too.

I was not telling my Mom about John because he was 21 years old. Yes! Nine years older than me.

As we began to get serious, John and I began to see each other every day. Every morning before school, he would ride his quad into town. I would sneak out of my house and go to his place on the farm before school. I was worried that he would leave me, so I thought if I saw him in the morning and had sex with him, he would not leave me or seek other women to be with.

At the age of 12, my concept of sex meant that I was the only love in his life.

I thought it was a perfect relationship, but my friends were still playing like a 12-year-old, playing and having fun, and I didn't have this anymore.

As time went on, I began to rebel against my Mom's rules, sneaking out at night to party, hanging around an older crowd.

Things began to heat up at these parties, and the hard drugs began to come out, and I was very curious. Seeing everyone around me injecting cocaine and heroin, I wanted to fit in and be just like them. And so I did.

A NIGHTMARE IN A CHILD'S EYES

The first time I tried hard drugs, I injected heroin. Scared and nervous but curious, as I sat there and watched them prep my "smash," my tummy had butterflies in it. Putting a rope around my bicep to make my veins pop out, Jake stuck the needle into my vein, pulled back on the syringe. He pushed the drug into my vein as the blood went into the needle and knew we hit a vein. The moment it hit my bloodstream; I experienced a tingling throughout my body. I began to have warmness flowing through my entire body, leaving me in a state of numbness, relaxed and feeling nothing at all. Nothing around me bothered me, and I just sat there in numbness.

My friends drifted away from me. Their parents didn't want them to do anything with me because of my behavior and the crowd I spent time with.

Losing my friends hurt me.

But I was so in love it didn't matter.

I later found out that John was sleeping with another girl a few years older than me. Let's call her Holly. Holly's Mom found out that this older man was having sex with her daughter and took it to the Police. John was arrested and charged with rape.

I was so in love with this man that I defended him.

I met with his lawyer at his parent's place and gave all the positive characteristics, lying that he had never done anything to me. In hopes, he would not be charged and sent to jail.

The courts found him guilty and sentenced him to time in jail. My heart was ripped apart, thinking, what am I ever going to do? The man of my dreams has been taken away from me. We spoke once on the phone, and he told me we could no longer talk or see each other and broke it off.

At the age of 13, my life shattered yet again, with the feeling of abandonment.

As time went on, I realized that he was not the one. I could not wait around for him to get out of jail and move on.

Most 13-year-olds were having sleepovers, playing with their friends, giggling, laughing, and having fun. I was hanging with the older crowd partying, getting high, and drinking alcohol. Everything they were doing; I was doing so that I fit in.

Continuing to have the same actions, sneaking out, rebelling, and not listening to my Mom at all, she told me one thing I did the opposite. Because of my behavior, my Mom could not handle me and reach out to social services, where I was placed into a group home with other kids with severe mental issues. This place was not me! I thought I was doing nothing wrong.

I remember sitting on my bed in the group home, sharing a room with this other girl. I was scared that something was going to happen to me there. I knew I was not in the right place.

I was scared, particularly of this younger boy, who had many episodes of losing his mind and being violent and mean to the caregivers. What if he loses his mind on me? What will he do to me?

Again, being here and thinking that my Mom doesn't love me anymore, that my Mom doesn't want me to be a part of the family, that she is just going to get rid of me and leave me in the care of someone else. What a bitch! I could not believe what she had done.

But only being there for a short period, my Mom decided to take me back into her care. She came to pick me up. I could not get out of there fast enough and was happy to leave.

Arriving back home, and continued to hang around the same people, partying all the time and not listening to my Mom. Always doing the complete opposite of what she wanted of me.

I went to my Dad's to spend Christmas with him and his girlfriend at the time, not knowing what was ahead. I got there and big news! Mom and Dad decided that I would not be coming home and that I would be living with him for the rest of the school year. I was pissed at my Mom again, this time feeling that she did not care about me. She keeps shipping me away because she can't handle me.

After finishing the school year at my Dad's, I went back home, and I was excited.

Now don't get me wrong, I enjoyed being at my Dad's, but I wanted to go back to my group of friends again. I missed partying and getting high. And just like that, I went back to my old ways until I was forced to live with my Dad.

Later, I met another man way older than me. Let's call him "Randal." We started dating, and it got serious.

At age 14, just shortly after I got my learner's license, Randal and I had a few friends over at my house while my Mom was at work. We were having some drinks after school, feeling good. I decided we needed more booze, so my girlfriend and I jumped in the car and headed uptown. I was driving, of course, and on the way back home, I decided to race someone and got myself into a car accident, where I just missed a tree, went through a fence, and into a garage, pushing the car inside the garage out the other side.

The Police showed up, and thank God my girlfriend, and I were not hurt, a bit shook up, and soon enough, I found myself charged with dangerous driving.

I attended court. I got a sentence of 18-months' probation, where I had rules to follow made by the law, a curfew, and to attend school.

At this time, Randall lived with his brother in town, and I remember sneaking out to see him, spending my non-curfew hours at his place, keeping it from my Mom.

THE DARKNESS THROUGH ADDICTION

At the age of 17, once probation was over, I decided to move in with Randall at his parents' store to finish my last year of high school.

Living with Randal, we continued to party, mostly consuming alcohol and having the occasional parties with opiates, mainly heroin and morphine.

Chapter Two
A Mom's Perspective: A New Beginning

My parents and three sisters moved to a big city when I was a little girl. We all started school there. My Dad worked on road construction, so he was not home most of the summer, and my mom took care of us then by herself. Dad would be home on weekends, and then there was lots of fun. We all would go to the fair together. Or we would go down by the river and have a picnic at the park with my grandmother.

In the winter, my dad was home, and he would make a skating rink for us in the backyard. He taught all of us how to skate. My Mom sewed our clothes for us, so we were always dressed the same. I didn't know that clothes could be bought from a catalog until I started school, and the other kids told me that.

My sisters and I were very close. We were always together. People used to say to my parents that something was wrong with us because we were so well-behaved and always cared for each other. When I was in sixth grade, my parents decided to move to a dairy farm. That was a shock. There were no more times to go to the fair or do things as a family. We learned how to work.

My parents got us all involved in 4H. We learned a lot about the type of cattle we raised and farm living. My parents became very involved with figure skating, and they started the figure skating club in the town that was close to our farm. So the skating skills that my Dad had taught us helped us with our figure skating.

THE DARKNESS THROUGH ADDICTION

A couple of years after moving to the farm, I became a rebellious teenager. If my dad said no, I said yes—most of the difficulties involved my dad. But the one thing that was important to me was school. I worked hard in school and had excellent grades when I graduated high school. I had always wanted to be a nurse, so I applied and was accepted, but then five months after graduating high school, I met a guy who became my husband. My new dream changed to being a good wife.

My husband and I moved many miles from my home. We moved that far away because of my husband's job. I was so glad for the phone because when I got homesick or needed to know how to do something, I could call my parents. My Mom was always my go-to person. She seemed to know precisely how my sisters and I thought and could help with everything. When I was growing up, I had felt that I would live close to my parents, and I could see them whenever I wanted. It was hard living that far from them. I had to learn things on my own. I even had to learn how to cook. My Mom would let us bake but never let us cook a meal.

So that was an experience for me and my husband. Some things were not good. But with time, I did get good at cooking. After my husband and I had kids, we moved to the farm. We both thought that would be a great place to raise our family. Little did I know how tough farm life would be. Interest rates were through the roof, and my husband ended up losing his job. We learned through hard work and to live on very little.

I remember moving to the farm. We built a new cedar log house and had a baby on the way. I was so excited at the thought of maybe having a girl since we had two boys. That spring, we had a baby girl. I was thrilled.

When Melissa was eight months old, she had an asthma attack and almost died. The first night that she was in the hospital, I overheard the doctors say that she would never make it through the night, but she did and got better. Melissa had quite a few

A MOM'S PERSPECTIVE: A NEW BEGINNING

attacks until school started. We often drove like crazy to the hospital because she couldn't breathe. Her Dad spoilt her after her first attack, and that was why she was daddy's little girl.

I thought farm life would be a great way to bring kids up. It was great for a few years. My husband had a fantastic job in town at the plumbing shop there. He made good money there, and on the side, we had hay that we could sell for extra cash. But then, one day, he got into his head to rent and buy more hay land. He wanted to farm for a living, but I knew that would be hard. Back then, the interest rates were unbelievable. We were paying 18% interest on our mortgage, and it was a floating mortgage, so our payments were high.

I found myself constantly praying we could meet our needs. I got my prayers answered. After returning from church, I would find money in my bible. No idea how it got there, but I was so grateful.

I also had a vast garden that supplied all of our vegetables. We also had pigs and sold the wiener pigs for a profit. So, with the extra hay land and the pigs and the time he spent doing this, he ended up losing his job. The farming life became hard and added more pressure.

I got a job in town at a restaurant cooking to help supplement our income. Even with the job in town, I continued doing everything I did on the farm before. It was a lot of work. And there were times my husband told me that I was not doing enough. So, I would push myself harder.

A year later, I got a job at a lodge. I fell in love with that job to the point that I took a course to become a PCA (nurse's aide). Helping and caring for senior people taught me so much. I would be up at five am to go to work, come home and go out and help in the barn with the pigs, then continue on my day with the baking, cleaning, and preparing meals. I also made all my kids' clothes. They, at times, got called the homemade kids.

THE DARKNESS THROUGH ADDICTION

In the winter, my husband started working for a tree-cutting company. He started drinking a lot at this time. I think it could have been the pressure of trying to make ends meet on the farm that drove him to that. The more he drank, the more miserable and mean he got. He started saying mean and terrible things to me.

There were times that I took the kids with me to work, and they would sleep in the quiet room. My husband had been drinking, and I was afraid that he would burn the house down because he smoked and maybe leave a lit cigarette burn. He pushed me away mentally, emotionally, and physically to the point that I chose to leave. I didn't like my kids hearing and seeing the fights and drinking.

At the time, I thought it was the right choice. I remember telling my Mom that I would leave, and she tried to talk me out of it. She said it would be hard on the kids because she knew what it was like to be the child of a divorced family. But I started to make a plan to move to town.

I rented a small house in the small town where we lived. I continued to work at the lodge. It was hard to make ends meet initially, but after a few months, we were doing fine. I was not getting any child support from my husband. But we were okay.

The kids' Dad would come on weekends and pick them up. He came to pick up the kids a few times, and he had been drinking, and I wouldn't let them go with him. I remember Melissa asking me to tell her Dad to stop drinking. I told her that I couldn't make him stop, that he had to do that himself. Then I found out that he was drinking all weekend when he had them. The kids didn't want to go there anymore, except Melissa. She was always a daddy's little girl. She visited him on weekends until he started working as a plumber in Inuvik, Northwest Territories. She did still go to see him when he was home.

After living in town for a year, I decided to see if I could find a job somewhere else. And start a new beginning: me and my kids.

A MOM'S PERSPECTIVE: A NEW BEGINNING

I went for an interview and landed a good job in another province. It was a long way away from my family and friends, but it would be a fresh start. Two weeks after my interview and getting the job, I moved to my new beginning place. It was easy to catch onto the job. It was like the one I worked on before. The only difference was new names and faces, but I loved that job. It was not a full-time job. It was a part-time job, but I could pick up extra if I needed it, which I did because I needed the money. I had left the kids behind with their aunt because the school year was not quite over when I moved.

I knew that they'd been taken care of, and I would have time to unpack and get our new home ready. It also gave me a chance to learn everything at work and get to know new people. And most of all, the opportunity to get caught up on sleep. I didn't realize how tired I was, working the schedule that I was working before. I worked days, evenings, and nights. So, when I went for the kids, I would be ready.

But I was not ready for what happened. I had no idea their Dad would be there. They hugged, cried, and sobbed when we got in the car. It was a long drive trying to console the girls, and finally, they stopped crying. I told them that their Dad would come to visit and that he would call them. I also told them that they would soon have new friends. And that they were fortunate because they would have friends from back home plus new friends. So they would have lots of friends.

My second son decided to stay with his aunt for most of the summer; then, two weeks before school, I had my oldest son (who was living at my parents' place as he was working in the same city that they lived in) bring him to Alberta so he could start school.

The girls seemed to enjoy the summer in the area where we lived. They met other kids that were from Saskatchewan and played with them. Melissa got a job babysitting and made herself some cash. After my son came, we talked about how we would make ends meet as I was only working a part-time job. That was why he didn't want to go and live there because he was afraid that we wouldn't have enough even to live. I told him that was my worry, not his. I knew how to work hard, and if I needed another job to make ends meet, I would do that. But to ensure that their Dad does his part, I went to Maintenance Enforcement to ensure that I would always have child support to help with the necessities of life for the kids. It wasn't much, but it helped.

Then school was about to start. We got all the new supplies and a couple of new outfits, and we were ready. So I thought. I will never forget that first day of school when I took them. They looked terrified. They all said it's so big and we don't know anyone. My son said, "I will never have friends." The fear I saw in their eyes was horrible. I got back into my car that day after taking each of them to their classroom and asking myself, "what have I done to my kids?" I felt guilty for moving my kids so far away from their home. I started to cry. I thought maybe they wouldn't have friends. Perhaps I made a mistake. Perhaps I should have stayed where I was.

When I picked them up, they were all quite happy and had met new friends. They all started doing sports which were one thing that they all enjoyed. Two weeks after my son was in school, he came home and said, " I finally have a life." Things were good for a while. Then all the trouble started.

Along with the good friends, also bad friends were found. Melissa found herself a boyfriend that was way older than her. He was an adult, and she was still a child. I wanted to find out if sex was involved in this relationship, so I took her to a doctor only to find out that the doctor couldn't tell me a thing. The law states that a child as young as 12 can consent to sex. What is wrong with the law? I could do nothing to keep him away. I even tried talking to him, but he smiled and drove away with my daughter in his vehicle.

One year after we moved, I got a full-time position at the Auxiliary Hospital. I decided it was time to buy a house. And, at this time, I met a man. He was a lovely man. He was so kind and didn't want to be a father but a friend to my kids, and he tried hard to do that.

If he asked Melissa to do something at home, she would say to him, "no, you're not my dad, and I don't have to." She was mean to him. But he was still good to all of them. And even then, he moved in with me. He also was a bit of a handyman and helped me fix the house. Of course, the place I found needed work.

Just after I moved into my new home, my parents came to visit, and when we were out looking at the backyard, and I was telling them everything that I was going to do in the yard, they noticed a little chair by Melissa's window. My Dad said to my Mom, "doesn't that remind you of something." I said, "she's climbing out the window." So, I went in and put a nail in the window so she couldn't open it. So, I thought, but there is a way when there is a will.

She worked at that thing all night and got it out, and she was gone. Now the trouble started. Melissa started sneaking out to be with her newfound boyfriend and bad friends. She became a party animal. I tried everything to get her to stop. I became so angry with her. "Why could she not just be a good kid?" Live by the rules in my house and be happy.

I was afraid that she would become an alcoholic, a high school dropout, or pregnant. I was so angry at her. Life would be so simple if she would just live by simple rules. Rules that were there to protect her. She couldn't understand why I was hard on her. I wasn't hard on her, I loved her so much, and she thought I hated her because of the rules I was trying to enforce.

I went for counseling, and they gave me ideas of things I could do to control maybe this kid that was out of control. But nothing worked. She would not live by any of my rules.

Then parents of Melissa's friend and I got together, and we had the guy charged, and he went to jail. After a bit of time, she forgot about him but continued a downward path. I had to get Social Services involved and have her put in a group home because she would leave home for days at a time, and I had no idea where she was.

I sure did not get any sleep at this time. I was under so much stress because of Melissa's behavior that I lost weight. But I continued to go to work and do a good job. My boss even said to me one day. "I don't know how you do such a good job here with everything that is going on in your home." I had learned a long time ago how to shut the home door when I went to work and open it when I got home. I did it somehow in my mind. I am very grateful that I learned that little mind-trick.

She got quite a bit better there, and I wanted to bring her home, but I had to fight for her. It seems Social Services decided that my home was not a good place for her to be. I fought long and hard for her, and she came home, but as time went on, she got worse and worse again. Christmas rolled around, and the kids always went with their Dad for Christmas only because he worked so far north and only came out then and once in the summer.

I had talked to my Mom on the phone, crying and crying. I didn't know what to do with Melissa. I wanted her to live with her Dad and his girlfriend. But he had said to me, "she's not that bad." He didn't believe a thing I told him about her. My Mom took it upon herself to call my ex-husband and say that she would die if he didn't keep her. My Mom also said that there has to be someone who will always believe in the kids no matter what. I thought that my kids would be good people with all my heart.

She stayed with her Dad. Melissa could only come back to me if she followed the rules. I stuck to my guns. She showed her true colors to her Dad. He then knew that everything I said was true. My ex-husband said to me one day that Melissa was so stubborn, just like me, and I told him that I knew that, but she needs to learn how to use her stubbornness for good to do well in life. Then we worked together, and she changed and moved back home with me six months later. We could talk to each other. And she could understand things between her Dad and me better.

All these things were going on in my home made this lovely and wonderful man in my life get sick. He started having stomach problems and was losing weight too. I could only do the right thing. I asked him to leave. I didn't want to see him get hurt any more than he was. We parted as friends.

At Easter time, when Melissa was home with me, she met a guy. They drank and partied, but it wasn't nearly as bad as before. I had sold Melissa's boyfriend a car, and one day when I was at work, I got a phone call from my youngest daughter. She was sobbing on the phone. Melissa was in an accident and had driven through a fence into someone's garage. Melissa ended up in court, and the court ruled that she take extensive driver training, and if she so much as got a parking ticket, her license would be pulled. They also ordered that she stay in school and have good grades.

Melissa had turned 16 that spring. Shortly after, she decided to move out and in with Randall. This guy was eight years older than she. We had a very long conversation about this, and she said to me, "I'm 16, and I can move out on my own if I want," And she did. She continued to go to school. Her grades were good, and she graduated from high school and moved to the city to go to college, became a legal assistant, and landed a great job. All this time, she was still living with Randall. They bought a house together and a reliable car. I was glad they got the car. And then they got married. To live happily ever after. Nope.

It wasn't long after they were married that they started doing things separately. Melissa liked to play sports and work out. She found friends that wanted to bike and go to the gym. Randall wanted to sit around at home and play video games. Melissa started going out with friends to the bars and seeing someone else. She ended up moving in with a guy she had met when she was out partying with friends.

THE DARKNESS THROUGH ADDICTION

At this time, I called Melissa and asked her if she would talk to her brother, who was into drugs. And try to get him to come and see me. He was on the road to destruction at this time. So Melissa went to talk to him, but it didn't play out how I thought it would. Melissa did bring her brother to my place, but little did I know what was going on. They both were on the road to destruction.

Because of the drugs, the new boyfriend Melissa had been living with kicked her out. Plus, she lost her job. She was down to nothing. Nothing except the drug world and all those friends. A very destructive path.

CHAPTER Three
Just When You Think Everything Was Going Right

Life was going well. I had graduated and headed in the right direction in life, well, so I thought. Randal and I decided to move to the big city to continue my education. Off to college, I went to get my legal assistant diploma.

During my time in college, Randall and I dabbled back into hard drugs here and there, mainly opioids, heroin, and alcohol. It was only weekend events where we would go and buy the drugs—usually having the dealer come over to our house, where we would all sit around injecting morphine or heroin.

I remember as the drug entered my bloodstream, it would give me a sense of a warm tingly sensation throughout my whole body. I would fully emerge into a state of relaxation. I was numb everywhere, and all my worries disappeared. We would all sit around nodding off, and I found myself running to the bathroom to puke at times. It was a common side effect of the drug.

Once I graduated from college and got my legal assistant diploma, I landed a good job and cleaned up. After four years of being a legal assistant, I decided to become a massage therapist. I enrolled myself in a course. I continued to work at the law firm I was at, and once I graduated, I landed an excellent massage therapist job and left my legal assistant career.

I felt I was on the right path in life. I loved to help people, and being a massage therapist is what I truly loved doing. This job led to purchasing our first home. And soon after, Randall asked me to marry him, and we started to plan the big day. As time went on, I didn't feel that love for him like I did before. On the day of our wedding, I thought I was doing the wrong thing in my heart. I expressed this to my grandma, and she said, "Don't be silly, Melissa. You're just getting the wedding jitters."

I remembered my conversation with my grandma on my wedding day as I walked down the aisle, putting on a happy face and fake excitement. But to be honest, I was more excited to get it over so that the party could begin.

After the wedding day, my feelings were fast drifting away, and we split up. I felt deep inside that I was married to my best friend, not my lover, nor someone I wanted to spend the rest of my life with.

Like really, I was with the man since I was 14 years old, and I felt as an adult that I was robbed of my childhood, never having the "teenage" experiences I should have had.

Upon splitting up, we lived together in the house we bought until I found somewhere to live. I continued to work as a massage therapist, and I found myself going out for drinks a lot more, just so that I didn't have to be in the same house as Randal.

As time went on, I met a man at the pub. We began to see each other more frequently at Karaoke events and chatted more. He had a beautiful voice and seemed to have it together.

As time went by, we began to date. I felt it was only suitable to move out of the house I was sharing with my ex-husband, and I decided to move in with him.

The new man I was dating was a kind and gentle fellow, but he was a social butterfly, and I found myself going out more frequently. Every night we would go to a pub where there was

JUST WHEN YOU THINK EVERYTHING WAS GOING RIGHT

karaoke so that he could sing. With going out came the consumption of alcohol, which began to be more frequent, as we now would go out every day of the week. I found myself back in that rabbit hole. This time I was staying up late and drinking.

I received a call from my Mom, her voice had a quiver, and I felt something was wrong. She said, "Melissa, can you please go get your brother and bring him back here."

My brother had been battling drugs for a while. His wife left him and took his daughter away due to his behavior and drug use. He just continued to get deeper into his addiction.

Being the good sister that I am, I said yes. Not knowing what was ahead of me, I jumped into my car and headed out of town to "rescue" him.

Arriving at this sketchy house, I was scared and nervous to go inside. It was rundown, not taken care of, doors falling off, window screens ripped, and an unkempt yard. Vehicles were all over, and kids' toys were lying around everywhere.

As I began to walk up to the house, I entered the house without knowing what to expect. It was a disaster. It was dirty. I don't think it had been cleaned in months. There was stuff all over the floor, dirty dishes everywhere, and the smell OMG, it stunk; it smelt like a BO and a mixture of chemicals and burning plastic, just like when you walk into a hair salon. The smell was so strong it was hard to breathe.

Then, I saw my brother and a few other people sitting around with crack pipes in one hand and a lighter in the other hand. They all looked like death. My brother looked like he hadn't showered or slept in days. I could see his pupils from across the room where I stood. On top of this, I was shocked at how much weight he had lost.

I stood there watching them all take a pull off their pipes, exhaling the smoke; so many thoughts were going through my head, don't give in, you got this Melissa, you can do this, get your brother, and get out as fast as you can.

I said to my brother, "Okay, let's go! I am here to pick you up. Mom wants me to grab you and take you to her house. She wants to chat with you." You could tell that was not something he wanted to do. I remember him saying to me, "No, I am not going anywhere. Why don't you have a hit?"

"What the FUCK!" was going through my head, "You want me to take a hit" absolutely NO WAY! Let's go; I cannot do that.

Anyway, all of them there in the room continued to ask me. I gave in and had a hit.

OMG ... I was in heaven and felt like I was on cloud 9. It was better than the drugs I had ever tried before.

As I inhaled the first-ever crack hoot, as I exhaled, I was already high and feeling that euphoric feeling it gave you. The rush was incredible throughout my whole body. It numbed any bad feelings I had and made me feel better. All my worries instantly faded, and I immediately became energetic and alert. It was a euphoric experience to feel my whole body become numb and so relaxed.

Seriously it was like ALL my worries and problems were gone. Every limb and muscle in my body relaxed, numb, and tingly. It was an erotic feeling. Something that I could get used to very fast.

The high began to wear off fast, like 5-10 minutes later, and I wanted more. I became anxious and uncomfortable. The sensations in my body were gone, which triggered me to want more. I didn't have that euphoric feeling anymore. I became jittery and anxiety set in. I was pacing, my heart was racing, and I could not keep my eyes off the floor. I kept looking to see if I could see a dropped crack hoot.

JUST WHEN YOU THINK EVERYTHING WAS GOING RIGHT

As the night went on, I found myself very high and not going anywhere. I just wanted to get even higher, and so I did.

I ended up going home in the early hours of the morning to avoid seeing my boyfriend. I also had to call into work and lie, telling them I was sick.

I remember sitting on the couch sketching out and wanting more, but I didn't have anymore. The drug wore off, and I was left there sitting alone in silence, thinking to myself, what have I done. I felt guilty, pissed off at myself, and like a failure. I was worried about what I was going to tell Mom because I knew this would upset her.

My boyfriend went on a trip with his family for an entire week, and this is when I hit it hard. I would meet up with my brother and his friends to get high. We went for days on end. No sleep, crack hoot after crack hoot. We were going from one house to the next house. Wherever the crack was, that's where we were.

When my boyfriend returned home, he knew something was up and that I had been doing something odd. He found out that I was using drugs and kicked me out.

With nowhere to go, I asked my ex-husband if I could move back in for a while. So, I did. Every night after work, I would hook up with my brother and his friend, and we would all get high.

I was still working as a massage therapist, and I remember being up all night getting high and having a crack hoot right before going to work. I was higher than a kite, but thinking I was acting normal, I was probably not in all reality.

There was a time during a massage session when I was so tired from not sleeping for days. I started to hallucinate during my client's session. Once, I saw a little girl in the room staring at me. It was odd and creepy. I was even nodding off during my session. It took all I had to get through them, always craving another hoot so it would wake me up as I was drifting away fast. It took everything I had not to fall asleep on my client.

I soon after was let go of my job, but in my eyes, that was perfect because now I could get high and hang out with my brother and his friends, as none of them had jobs. They just got high.

I started spending a lot of my time with this tattooed guy. We began to date and fall in love. I got a place in a small town where we moved in together.

At that time, I was still not working and living off my credit into my addiction. My addiction was so bad that I consumed an ounce a day, so I started selling drugs to support my habit.

I was introduced to some of the "Big Guys" in the city, where I would drive up every couple of days to reload. My customers were all over the province, putting a lot of kilometers each day. I did this all hours of the night and day.

There were days I had been up for more than three days at a time. I felt so popular because my phone was going off so much, people needed me, and I was making enough money to support my habit. There were also times that I would end up smoking all the drugs I bought instead of selling them, my credit started to deplete very fast.

With me selling drugs and driving all over the countryside, there were times, actually many times, I would rent a hotel room and sell out of the hotel room, and other times I would just sell out of my house, just really depending on where I was. I felt like I was a high roller because I would rent hotel rooms and fancy cars to do my deliveries.

You see, I thought I was "playing" with the Police because they would not know it was me. I truly felt indestructible and invisible and thought I was clever by fooling law enforcement. But at the same time, I was so paranoid that the Police were watching me, and this was a way to "trick them," LOL, so I thought.

JUST WHEN YOU THINK EVERYTHING WAS GOING RIGHT

I remember staying in a hotel this one time, taking the night off from selling, of course, getting high. My boyfriend, let's call him George, and I plus another man, were there. George and I went into the bathroom to shoot up together.

After taking that injection, I was so scared. Once it hit me, which was instant, I began to feel as if the room was going in circles. I felt extremely hot and flushed. I knew I took way too much, thoughts going through my head, "OMG! I am going to die right here right now. I will never be able to see my family again, my Mom, my Dad, and my siblings." I was beyond scared.

I grabbed onto the sink, hugging it and trying not to spin away, but literally, my body was going back and forth, and all I kept saying was, "Melissa, you got this, you are not going to die, you are not going to die." It was a scary moment as I thought it was my time.

The high started to wear off, and I didn't need another smash for a while after. But as it wore off, I hit the pipe again, wanting that feeling to come back.

Smoking an ounce of crack a day made me feel "normal" when I was high cause I didn't know anything different. I didn't know what it was like to be sober.

If and when I went to sleep, I would have to have my crack sitting beside me in the pipe, ready to hit when I woke up.

Crack was the first thing I thought of when I woke up and the last thing I thought of right before I went to sleep (when I did). I could not stand not being high. The moment I woke up, I wanted that numb feeling to penetrate my body, making all my problems diminish. So when I did finally go to sleep, which was about on average every three days, I would sleep for hours, sometimes days.

Injecting cocaine was another way I liked to get high, and I did that from time to time. Usually, when I reloaded and got cocaine from the dealer before cooking it up, is when I found myself injecting, and minutes later, I would be taking a pull off the pipe.

One afternoon as some buddies and I were sitting around at my house. I was getting my "smash" ready to inject, and again after injecting, I knew it was too big again. I hit the floor this time and did the "chicken," but luckily, I could come out of it. You see, as your body gets so used to being so high for so long, you begin to think that you need to start doing bigger ones so that you can get high.

George and my relationship got more serious, but at the same time, it got weird. He was a man who had a lot of insecurities and had been cheated on in prior relationships. I think the drugs and being high so much started to get to his head. He began to get weird, to the point that he thought I was cheating on him if I was talking to another guy. If I spoke to another man and looked them in the eyes, I was sleeping with them. It got to the point that I had to look down and not make eye contact with any other guy as I spoke to them. It was very uncomfortable, but I didn't want to set him off.

As the days and months went on, it got worse. George got angry more often. The look on his face was terrifying, his eyes wildly, one pupil would get dilated, and one would get constricted. When this happened, I knew I was in for a fight.

The fights involved yelling with a lot of emotional abuse and began to get physical. It was pushing, holding me down or up against the wall, and shouting in my face.

One afternoon, we decided to go to a tattoo convention in the big city as we had to get picked up in any event. Before we headed out of town, we stopped at this woman's house. She asked us if we wanted to try this drink. The drink had crystal meth in it. Of course, George had it, so did I.

I drank it up, and we headed to the city. I remember driving my car down the highway when it suddenly hit me. The vehicles

JUST WHEN YOU THINK EVERYTHING WAS GOING RIGHT

going by me in either direction looked like lightning bolts going by, and it got so bad that I had to pull over on the highway.

I had no idea what was going on, but I was not too fond of it. I could not drive anymore and traded spots. I don't remember much after that.

But when we got to the convention, I entered the building, and all I remember was getting to the doors to enter, and I said to George, I can't go in; my senses in my ears were so clear, like crystal clear that I could hear everyone's words around me.

I thought I was overdosing. I knew I needed help ASAP but did not want to admit it. I went to the front counter and told the lady at the desk that I needed an ambulance now as I fell and hit my head.

She called the ambulance, they arrived and brought me in. I remember lying on the bed, floating up, looking down at myself as the paramedics worked on me to save my life. What an experience this was! I had always heard about it but never believed it. I saw the paramedics working on me, calming me down and telling me that I would be okay. I thought to myself, well, now I did it; God will take me this time.

Later that morning, I was discharged, and George came to pick me up. The first thing I did was have a crack shot to take the edge off and get me feeling back to "normal" again.

We continued down the path of using and getting even deeper into it than we were before.

I remember one day when we were out delivering drugs and stopped at someone's place. We grabbed some booze and headed over to have some drinks and get high. As the night went on, things got heated. I am not sure why this was, but George got violent with me. He hurt me to the point that I had to go to the hospital.

THE DARKNESS THROUGH ADDICTION

George was arrested and charged with assault. He had to attend court, and I was fearful that he would go to jail. I didn't want him in prison as he was the man I loved despite him mistreating me.

I know, silly, right? How could you love someone that hurt you, mentally and physically, day in and day out?

He got sentenced to spend time in jail, and I continued to live my everyday life, getting high and selling drugs.

Shortly after losing our house, we got our eviction notice, so I packed everything up and moved it to my ex-husband's house.

After this, my younger sister opened her door to let me stay with her as I had nowhere to go. I was pretty rough; I did not sleep, shower, eat, or brush my teeth for days when I got there.

For the first few days, I slept. I remember all I did was wake up to go to the bathroom, have a quick bite to eat and drink, then go back to bed. I felt like shit, actually more like death. I was so weak. My body ached all over, my mouth was dry, and I had the worst headache ever.

Being out of drugs and knowing I had no money even to get some, I just kept going back to sleep. The withdrawals were unbearable. The anxiety was setting in because all I wanted was to get high, and not knowing when and how I was going to cause me a lot of anxiety.

My cravings for drugs were stronger. I wanted it but could not have it. My mood swings were outrageous, and I am sure my sister was done with me. I would lose my marbles for no reason.

I was restless and just wanted to sit or sleep. When I stood to go to the bathroom, my body was so weak, and I was wobbly and light-headed. It was like darkness was always around me.

I became stronger from getting some sleep, rest, and food in my belly.

JUST WHEN YOU THINK EVERYTHING WAS GOING RIGHT

I decided to steal my sister's money and get high. It was not even that much, but it was enough to get me a few hits.

At this point, this was the only way I would be able to get high because I had lost everything. All I had was my car and the garbage bags full of clothes. My money was gone, credit cards maxed out. I had no money to get drugs to sell them. I was at rock bottom. So, stealing money from her was the only way I supported my habit.

After catching on that I was stealing from her, she kicked me out, leaving me no place to go. I had to get this figured out and back on my toes. I got some drugs fronted me to continue to stay high because I got anxious when I had none. After all, I had to be high every waking hour I was awake and, of course, in the meantime.

Having built some money up from selling, I began to stay in hotels again, bouncing every couple of days, to avoid the hotel managers catching on to me.

It was near Christmas, George was still in jail, and my sister was going to my Dad's place up North, she asked me to come along with her, and I decided to.

We ended up leaving in the evening because I was waiting for my drugs to be delivered to the hotel. I kept lying and making excuses why it took me so long to come out of the hotel. Finally getting my cocaine uncooked, I quickly cooked some up for the drive. I pulled out the baking soda, spoon, water, and lighter. I began to cook my crack. She picked me up, and we headed out.

Away we went!

I would ask her many times to stop, lying to her that I needed to stop so I could pee or have a smoke or whatever excuse I made, hiding it from her that I needed to get high.

THE DARKNESS THROUGH ADDICTION

She was getting frustrated with me and just wanted to continue as it was getting super late. We arrived at my Dad super late.

I was strung out and high, which was the norm for me. I had to be high all the time. The next day we visited, and I remember needing to get high. I used the bathroom to shoot up because it was easier than smoking crack, and there would be no smoke.

I don't remember much more of the time there as it was all a blur for me. But that evening, as everyone was sleeping, I remember sitting by the sliding door in a chair with a book and pen in hand as I wrote George in jail.

I sat there, and every 5-10 mins, I would light my pipe and get high, blowing the smoke out the door.

Shortly after Christmas, George got out of jail and went to a treatment center. We stayed in contact, and he was about to be released, and I went to pick him up.

Driving the long drive and, of course, getting high along the way, I arrived to pick him up. The first thing he wanted was a hit.

We began to drive back to my hometown, drifting off to the backroads so we could get high. The more we got high, the more George got sketchy. He started getting weird and said, "Stop, pull over!" And the argument started. He thought I had someone in the vehicle with me. He had me pull over and rip my car apart to the point where he took out the seats in the back and the liner in the trunk.

Scared, nervous, and not knowing what he would do to me left me on edge.

I kept assuring him that it was just us. I tried to stay as calm as possible so that he didn't get even more pissed off. He was paranoid. I was just going along with whatever he wanted me to do. I honestly didn't know if he would kill me or not. We were out in the middle of nowhere. I was terrified, my heart was beating so fast, and all I could do was get high as he was yelling and ripping my car apart.

He cooled down after realizing there was nobody in the car, and we headed down the highway. After this experience, we decided to clean up to save our relationship.

My Mom opened her door to us, and we stayed with her for a bit as we figured things out. Then, we decided to stay with his parents in a small town in another province.

We headed out to start over, a new life being clean.

We moved into his parents' farmhouse, cleaned up, and later I landed a waitress job and began to work while George helped his Dad around the farm. We were doing good, got ourselves cleaned up, and felt like something good was happening for us.

After a while, we decided and thought we could go and pick up, do it just once, and be good. Little did we know, and should have known, as an addict, you can't just go and use once and then stop.

So, we did. We headed to the city, got a hotel, and picked up. And of course, no brainer, this began to become more frequent.

I remember the last time we went to the city and returned to the farm with drugs in hand. George was acting all weird, back to how he treated me when we used heavily. Always thinking I was up to something or thinking I was sleeping around on him. Things got heated that night, we were both high, and George insisted that we have sex, but I didn't want to, so right away, he thought I was sleeping around on him; he grabbed me and forced himself on me, and picked me up by my neck and pushed my back onto the wall.

The look in his eyes was terrifying. His left pupil dilated as the right one was as big as his eye. It looked like he was ready to kill me. I was shaking, crying, and so scared of the unknown. Throwing me onto the bed and pinning me down, punching me, I was trying, and it took all I had to try to fight him to get out of the house and run for help. All that was on my mind is I would be one of those girls who tried to fight for their lives and got killed. All I wanted to do was get free and run out that bedroom door up the stairs and run as fast as I could to find help.

He finally settled down and let me go.

The next day I went into work, having so much makeup on my face to try and cover my bruises; my boss asked me, "what happened?" and I explained I would never forget what he said, and that was "There may never be a next time that you get our safe and alive." And that stuck with me.

But it wouldn't be the last time. It happened again, things got heated, and the fighting continued.

I called my Mom, crying and wanting her to get me cause I was done with the abuse. I wanted out and wanted nothing to do with George. She drove all the way to pick me up, and I returned to my Mom's place.

Chapter Four
The Nightmare Begins

At this time, Melissa met yet another guy that she thought was Mr. Right. The guy gave me the creeps. He had tattoos all over him, and he was a tough-looking dude. They went about their lives doing drugs and dealing. Then one day, they ended up at my place. They had decided that they wanted to go to his parent's place in another province, miles away, and get clean. That would be wonderful if they did.

They did end up getting there in this old beater of a vehicle. How did they make it? It was beyond me. Yes!, I gave them money for gas. Did they use it for that? I don't know.

I was always giving the kids money for something. Sometimes it was to keep them alive because if they didn't pay up...... their life would be over for owing for their drugs.

They did make it to Mr. Right's parents' place and stopped doing drugs for a while. He went into treatment for some time but quit partway through. Melissa went to see him on his first-weekend pass, picked him up, and started using again. They went to visit my parents that weekend. I couldn't believe they did that. I remember my Mom saying I don't know where Melissa finds these guys. They give you the creeps. But my Mom still welcomed them in and fed them.

Melissa got a job in a restaurant. The owner of the place liked her. He started noticing that she had bruises on her. So, he talked to her about them. He told her one day that she should leave this guy. Around that time, I got a phone call in the night. All I heard was someone screaming, and I could listen to him beat Melissa.

I froze. I couldn't move a muscle as the tears flowed down my face. My biggest fear was that I would have the Police on my doorstep in the morning telling me that Melissa had been beaten to death or became invalid and had to be taken care of for the rest of her life. I started to pray for her. "Please, dear God, keep her safe and don't let her die," I said.

What could I do?

I could hear my daughter being beaten up by this guy. And there was nothing I could do. The phone was a pay-as-you-go, so the number didn't display on my caller id.

The next day she called me from the guy's parents' place, and she wanted me to come and get her. I got directions and left immediately. And wouldn't you know it by the time I got there, she didn't want to leave. After taking her for a drive around that town with this guy's mother talking sense to her, she decided to come home with me.

We had to go back to his place to get her car, but after talking with the guy's Mom, she decided that he and Melissa both needed help but alone. Melissa came back with me but didn't stay with me long. She was gone again.

She met up with newfound friends again and a few old ones. I figured out by this time that she was dealing drugs and living high. Weeks and months went by before I would see or hear from Melissa. She would stop by from time to time to talk. It was as if she needed to keep in touch with me. She was busy with her life. I started working lots during this time. It kept my mind on something else rather than worrying all the time about my kids.

I thought things should get easier after your children leave home, but mine seemed worse. There was always that gnawing in

THE NIGHTMARE BEGINS

the back of my mind, "where is she and what is she doing? Does she have food, and is she safe? It wasn't like the kids were teenagers. They were all young adults with their whole lives ahead of them.

CHAPTER Five
Handcuffs and shackles

"Life can be an uphill battle, but the more you keep pushing, the more hills and obstacles you keep climbing the stronger you will become"
~Anonymous

After arriving at my mom's house, I was back on the streets. I headed downtown to where all the drug addicts hung out so that I could hook up and get high. I shortly after that began to sell drugs again to support my habit.

At this point in my addiction, I would say I was homeless, living on the streets with nowhere to go. I had lost everything. I would find myself going from house to house, wherever I could stay and hang out so I could stay warm and dry. There was even a time when I went back and stayed at my ex-husband's place when there was nowhere else to go, just so that I could be somewhere warm during the cold winter months.

During this phase of my journey, I ran out of drugs, had none, and was desperate to get high. I would go to the extremes to get it, stealing from others.

I used my ex-husband a lot and "borrowed" money from him when I ran out.

I met another man, let's call him Tim. This man was a bit different than the others I dated. He was a criminal, in and out of jail most of his life, but he knew how to sweet talk women. He was good at that for sure. His voice and the words he used to persuade you and I found him very attractive.

Immediately he made me feel loved and cared for. He would open doors for me and get me things when I wanted them. He always made me feel important. As well, this was a more challenging time in my journey because I didn't always have money or drugs, and he knew how to get drugs when you had no money, and I later learned that involved some hefty stealing, in the beginning, he would say I will be back in a bit, and he would come back with food and drugs.

We began hanging out. Tim always knew a way to get drugs when you had no money for them, and this is something I desperately needed because I was always running out.

Being with him was never a dull moment. We were always up to no good and into some trouble. One of his "specialties" was theft. We stole things from vehicles, quads to utility trailers, bobcats, you name it, he would spit it out, we would make a plan, and we would go on a mission to get it, which got me into trouble a few times, by getting busted and charged with theft. I took a case for him one time, so he didn't go to jail.

Another time, we spotted a running vehicle outside a store. The person left the truck running and doors open, a perfect score for us. Yup, we jumped in and drove away! Now, what a rush this was for me. I stole things before in my life but not to this extreme. The thrill and endurance that ran through my body were indescribable.

Another time we again were in a stolen truck and needed gas, so we stopped and filled up and frantically drove away without paying. Well, the store called the police, and the race was on.

Yup, it turned into a full-on police chase!

I held on for dear life – scared and shitless on the passenger seat – as we were going at 160 kilometers. We drove on gravel roads as the cop cars chased us. We entered a field and raced through the bumpy areas. Almost losing control at times, we finally came to a stop down where the cops could not see us. We escaped out of the truck and ran into the woods.

Now talk about adrenaline going through your body, and all I could think about was a hit of crack to calm me down, to numb me. We reached a spot where we could hide under some bushes. We sat there getting high and listening for the police, hearing helicopters above searching for us. It was terrifying, and I had no idea what would happen.

Hours had passed, and they were no longer looking for us. We could not hear anything, and the helicopters were gone. We began to head to the road to get reception and call someone to pick us up.

We continued this wild journey of drugs, sex, and rock and roll.

One evening we had managed to round up some money to get a couple of hits. So, we headed over to pick it up. We ran into the police on our way there, and they turned their lights on. Tim tried to outrun them in the vehicle, but we came to a dead-end shortly into the chase. He said, "okay, babe, we got to run meet you at the house. I love you!" and we were off on foot, outrunning the police, but I was not fast enough and was taken down to the ground and handcuffed and take me into custody. I had a warrant out for my arrest, so I knew I was done.

That night, I was sent to the remand center, where I awaited my sentence. They fingerprinted me, took my mug shot, and placed me in my cell. There I was in my cell surrounded by only four cement walls and a toilet off to the corner, lying on a small foam mattress. Heck, I wouldn't even call it a bed more like a foamy, with no blankets, cold, hungry, and very uncomfortable.

So many thoughts went through my head. Wow, was I scared and extremely fearful of what was about to happen? Yes. I didn't want to go to "jail," that's where all the criminals are, people that murder and do horrible stuff. That was not me!

Tim was caught shortly after me, and due to his lengthy criminal record, he was charged and remained in remand as he awaited sentencing.

It was time for my sentencing hearing.

The day came where I was transferred from JAIL in handcuffs on my arms and feet. I got placed into the back of the prisoner transport vehicle. It was full of other inmates that were being transported. And away we went down the highway in my tiny cell, chained up. It was time to pay off the money I owed for the warrant out for my arrest.

As I sat there, I pretended and showed the other inmates that I was strong and just like them. Deep inside me, I was shaken and horrified to go to jail with the "big guys," scared of the unknown or what would happen to me in there. All I knew about prison was what I had seen on TV, which was terrifying to me.

Before going into the actual jail, they handed me my inmate uniform and told me to put it on and leave my clothes with them.

And then it was time to enter the jail and be placed in my cell. I was terrified.

Heart racing, palms sweaty, lump in my throat, and not knowing what I was in for, the guards escorted me to my room, and as I began to walk through the jail, everyone stopped and stared at me. I was so uncomfortable, anxious, and fearful.

All I remember is it was huge, with really high ceilings. It was a two-story cellblock and the out circumference of the building with doors controlled by the guards. It was bright, carpeted with one large bathroom that all the inmates had to share, one large dining area where all the inmates ate together.

HANDCUFFS AND SHACKLES

Other inmates were walking around, reading, writing, cleaning, and visiting other inmates. It was nothing like I expected.

There were specific times during the day when we were locked up in our cell, "punishment time."

If we were not locked up or doing our chores (that is how I paid off my fine), we could roam around and do what we wanted, which there were not too many options.

I would be allowed to make a phone call from time to time, in which I always called either my mom or my dad. Those calls were hard because I didn't want to be in jail. I felt like I was being held captive and controlled by someone else.

The hours where I was locked in my cell were when I would lay on my cot and do a lot of thinking. I think of Tim and what that would look like when we both get out of jail. The thoughts of getting high made the days long. I just wanted to be high so bad. The feelings of being alone, being scared, not knowing what day or how much longer I had to be in there created a lot of anxiety.

Jail is not a place you want to be.

I had been in jail for about three weeks and had a little more time to go, but it was nearing Christmas, and I wanted out. I remember calling dad and asking him to bail me out. I knew he didn't want to, but I begged him to pay the rest of my fine, and he did. I used the guilt trip of wanting to be home for Christmas, but seriously that was the last thing on my mind. I just wanted to get back to the streets to get high. He agreed to pay my fine, picked me up, and drove me back to my home base.

I continued to see Tim while he was in jail, write to him, and visit him once per week in remand.

After jail, going right back to my ex-husband's place, over time, this house was becoming a drug house, people coming and going all the time.

I remember we were all sitting around getting high one night, and the police broke down the door and raided the house. The squad team came in from the front and back door, yelling, "Get down on the floor."

I went back to jail but was let go later that night as they didn't have anything to charge me.

After the raid, Randal and I decided to put the house up for sale, and it sold quickly.

By this time, Tim had served his time and was released. We decided to move to another province to be closer to his son. We wanted to start a new life and get away from the shit show in my home base city. So money in hand from the sale of the house, we loaded up all my stuff and off we went, to start a new life, well so we thought.

Immediately getting settled in, Tim and I met up with some of his old friends from the area and started to dabble back into drugs. It was nice to have money in hand and not steal to get high.

Over time, money had run out, which led us back to theft, stealing oversized items like Skidoos and quads with large utility trailers. We would take the stolen items and head back to the home base to sell them off to get money for drugs. We got caught, and he went back to jail, this time for a year.

I was out of jail that night because Tim took all the charges. His mom came and picked me up and took me into her home. We had a long conversation, and I decided to go to treatment.

She helped me get into a treatment center. Honestly, I didn't know if this was what I wanted; all I did know was what I needed. Going in my attitude, I will be clean for 28 days and have a safe and warm place to stay.

On my arrival at the center, I was pretty nervous; seeing all these other addicts there trying to get help made me feel a bit better.

The first week was the longest week EVER. That clock could not move fast enough. I would pace back and forth, going through withdrawals, sweating, shaking, and so moody. I was so restless that I couldn't sleep at night. I didn't want to be there. I just wanted this nightmare to end.

As my mind became clearer, the feelings of shame and guilt began to set in as I thought about all who I had hurt, who I had let down, who I pushed away from me.

Then the day came. I marbled out of treatment. I completed my 28 days. I was smiling from ear to ear and so proud of my accomplishment. Twenty-eight days clean and sober felt pretty amazing. I overcame some significant obstacles while in treatment and thought I was on the road to recovery. I remember standing up receiving my marble from my counselor in front of my family was a pretty spectacular moment.

Once I completed treatment, I decided to live with my aunt in the same city where Tim was serving his time.

Things were going amazing, being clean felt pretty good, and seeing life differently. I continued to stay with my aunt, which was pretty awesome. She opened her door to me and gave me the love and support I needed during the next few months ahead. I am forever grateful for that.

During this time, I would visit Tim in jail on the weekends, he was doing great, and we were happy to see each other.

I got a great job at a law firm and was delighted to find such a great place to work. I was pleased; I finally had my life back together, with things moving in the right direction.

THE DARKNESS THROUGH ADDICTION

Well, so I thought – again.

Tim was about to be released, and we were planning on our next move, getting a place together, so I searched and found one right across the street from my aunt's house, which I thought would be perfect.

Tim began to get weekend passes. He would come and stay at our new place and return on Sundays. Things were going well the first few passes, but then one weekend, he was released, and I decided to go pick him up. That was the end of my sobriety, and I began to go down that rabbit hole again. Tim never returned when his pass was up, and now he was on the run.

I got kicked out of that apartment and let go of my job. Things were going downhill very fast, and I found myself right back to where I was a year ago.

After being on the run for a while, we were stopped and arrested. My jeep got impounded, and we were taken into custody for the stolen items we had in the jeep.

Here I go again, back to jail and not knowing what would come out of this one, but the police didn't charge me. All the charges were on Tim.

The police called my mom to see if she would let me back into her care. They were going to pay for my bus ticket to head back to my home base. And away I went, big garbage bag in hand, onto the Greyhound bus back to reality.

Being at my mom's place for a while, getting things in order, I had applied for employment insurance and got some money in the mail; Yay!! Now I can get my jeep out of the impound.

There I was back on the Greyhound, money in hand, headed to get my Jeep out of the impound. I intended to get my jeep and head back to Mom's to get clean again.

But that little voice in my mind kept saying, "go pick up, go pick up." And what did I do? I listened to that little voice in my head, went to my old dealer's place, and got some crack for the drive home. About 2 hours away from home, I ran out of crack, and I was sketching out and feening for more. I began to call up some old friends in that area I was about to drive through and stopped by to grab some drugs. Well, it is needless to say, I didn't make it back to my Mom's.

Chapter Six
This Is, Really, A Nightmare

Around this time, I moved to the city to a job that was definitely for me. I loved the job. I worked in a very fast-paced part of the hospital. I met a few people just like me. They had problems with their kids. These were people that I could talk to, and they understood me. I started to go to Alanon, which was just what I needed. By going to these meetings, I realized that I was powerless over addiction and that my life had become crazy. And that a Power greater than me could restore me to sanity. To me, that Power I will call God.

I made new friends at these meetings that were like me. I was learning how to take care of myself. Something I had never done before. I was always taking care of some other person.

I even remember one day Melissa calling and wanting to know what I was doing. I had told her I had something to eat to get ready to go to work. She said something about "that being nice" that I could eat and that she was sitting on the side of the road and hungry.

I told her to get an f....ing job and hung up on her. I remember thinking, "it's easy; stop what you are doing. That's all you have to do." I had never done that before. For the first time in a long time, I felt like I had some power back. I felt stronger than her and courageous because I stood up for myself.

THE DARKNESS THROUGH ADDICTION

When I first started working in the city, I worked half time there and half time in the town I lived. And when I went back to town, I would also work at Tim Horton's after finishing my shift at the hospital.

One day this hard-looking girl came in and said, "Hi Mom, how are you?" I didn't even know my daughter. She was so thin and looked over 40, not 20. My heart sank. I quickly turned around and said, "I'm good." And I walked away.

I knew if I stood there any longer, I would start to cry. I didn't even know my daughter – my flesh and blood – and I was embarrassed to admit that she was my daughter. She looked horrible. And anyone would see that she was a heavy drug user. She had told me she was in town visiting some friends. Sure, she was there seeing "friends."

On one of my days off from work, I was cleaning my apartment, and after I was done, I sat on the couch to take a break. I heard on the radio about a man that had been murdered and that they had someone in protective custody until they could find the murderer.

In my heart, I knew that the person they were keeping safe was Melissa. I just knew. Mother's intuition, I guess. It wasn't a half-hour later I got a call from the police asking me if I knew this person and I confirmed that she was my daughter. They asked me to come to the police station to ask me some questions. They wanted to know if Melissa would tell the truth if asked something.

I said my daughter Melissa, the straight one, would never lie, but the druggy Melissa would lie. They asked me if I could tell the difference. Of course, I could. They asked me if I would go into a room with her and ask her specific questions regarding the murder and if I would know if she was telling me the truth.

So I went into the room and again I couldn't believe this person sitting there was my daughter. Melissa's appearance has changed so much. I was heartbroken when I saw her. She was a broken kid. Deep in my heart, I knew that she needed help, and I couldn't fix her. She needed professional help.

She was on her way to death if she kept going on the way she was going. She had significant weight loss. Melissa's hair was brittle and dried out bleach blonde. I was afraid her hair would break right off if I touched it. Also, her skin was dry. Her eyes were sunk in and had no shine to them, and her cheeks were sunken in and hollow.

My daughter's hands had lost their gentle and soft touch. Her fingers stained black from using crack and fingernails full of dirt – like if she had been weeding a garden. That's how dirty they were!

She was wearing light blue ripped jeans, a shirt, and a pink baseball cap on backward. She was jittery with fear, and her body was jerking around uncontrollably. And all the time she talked to me, she looked down at the table.

She told me how two guys came into this place she was at, and one guy lifted a gun and shot the guy sitting beside her. She told me how she heard the guy wheeze and take his last breath. She told me the two guys who came to shoot this guy had Skidoo toques on, and only their eyes could be seen. I asked all the questions the police wanted answers for, and she gave them. The one answer to a question she gave me was, "I will never forget that person's eyes that shot that guy."

This was more than I could take. I got up, walked out, stopped at the desk, and said, "Whatever she tells you is the truth. Listen to her." I was shaking like crazy when I walked outside to my car. I could not believe what I saw and what I heard. I thought that was the last time I would ever see my daughter. The thought of the kinds of people she was hanging out with made me sick to my stomach, and the tears started to run like a river. I had a great weight on me, and I couldn't get it off. The police kept her in protective custody for a few days. From there, who knows where she went.

THE DARKNESS THROUGH ADDICTION

Her dad's brother passed away about this same time, and my youngest daughter and I went to the funeral. I had to tell their dad about the murder. He and my youngest daughter hugged and hung onto each other, saying, "What will happen to her?" I turned and walked away. I was heartbroken too, and I cried and cried.

Shortly after the funeral, my youngest daughter got very sick. She had a psychotic breakdown and ended up in the hospital to get help. The doctor had told me that everyone has a breaking point, and she went over hers. I kept asking myself, what would this happen to her?

It was like she was a lost soul. I went to see her as much as I could, living across from the hospital and working there. I saw her lots. She had grand councilors and an excellent doctor. So, with all that and the right meds, she got well. She got a good job and moved in with her girlfriend. I was so happy about that. I also was so lost, and I needed her.

Melissa needed a place to stay, so I let her move in with me. It was only for a short time because she had a problem with rules. She was told that nobody could come to my place. Well, to my horror, one day, I came home from work, and my apartment was full of people. She invited all her friends. They ate all my food, and they each had a shower and got cleaned up, even using my razor to shave their faces. I screamed at them to get out, including Melissa. I found out later that they also stole money that I had hidden. They know where everything is.

It was starting to get cold out, and the snow was falling. I would go to my window and look out and wonder where Melissa was. The tears would stream down my face, and I would pray that God would protect her and keep her safe.

Shortly after the snow started falling, I got a phone call from Melissa. She was in jail. She was crying and crying that she wanted me to bail her out. Sorry, it was not happening. She would call collect every day, wanting me to help her. She did the crime; she could do the time. I knew she was safe in jail. I had a feeling of relief that she was in prison. I knew where she was. I knew she was eating, but she also got sick there, confined to an area. She was out of the cold and in a warm place. I stopped taking all the collect calls as I could not afford that, but I sometimes let her call.

She had told me one day that the guards in the jail said she didn't belong there. They said that they knew she was raised differently than most women there. I told her that she didn't belong in that place and she was better than that. But she had called her Dad, and he helped her get out. She was supposed to meet him at my place at Christmas, but she didn't show up. She reunited with a new boyfriend, and he was one of many crimes.

Since the weather was getting very harsh, with freezing temperatures and snow, Melissa needed a warm place to move in; so she went back into her ex-husband's house. She brought along her boyfriend, and they did and dealt drugs for money. The house had become a drug house. The house was trashed. Then, the police raided it one day. Her ex-husband came to see me, and I had told him that he had to quit helping her. He was like me.

He thought he could maybe save her. She needed to save herself. So the house was cleaned out and put up for sale. They each made a profit of $30,000. Melissa knew what she would do with her money, so she asked me if I would put it into a bank account in my bank. So, I did. I was going to do everything I could to keep the money because I knew in my heart that she would quit the drugs one day.

She and the new boyfriend moved to another province. They loaded up all Melissa's furniture and belongings, and they set off to a new beginning. They had told me that they were going to stop using drugs. Things sounded promising for a while. Then one day, she needed money. So, I sent a money order to her. The next thing I knew, she was here wanting more money. I took it out and gave it to her. She is mean when she uses, and I was scared of her and him. She kept asking for more and more until it was all gone.

The next thing I knew, there were more crimes and more crimes. Melissa was taking raps for him. Then they were on the run. But he got caught and went to jail. Melissa called his mom, and she said she would help her on one condition that she go for help. Melissa went to treatment, and his mother put all Melissa's belongings in storage.

She got assistance from the government to go to treatment. When she was in therapy, I was happy to talk to her. Melissa sounded like a normal person – the Melissa I knew. I went to her marbling out ceremony. I was so delighted that now things would be normal again. But, Melissa and her boyfriend communicated by phone while he was serving his sentence, and she decided to move to BC. She called my sister to see if she could live there with her. And she could, so she loaded up her jeep, and off she went.

On the way out there, I got a call from her. My heart sank. I thought, here we go again, but as it turned out, her vehicle quit working. She needed a battery. So I called the Canadian Tire where she was, and I bought her a new battery. They installed it, and she was on her way again. It seemed like an eternity before she got to my sister's, but she made it.

She did very well there. She got a job at a law office. My sister is a great person to talk to, so Melissa spoke to her about all kinds of things. My sister even taught Melissa about fashion. She learned how to dress up on a few dollars, in fact, clothes from the second-hand store. They used to go there on Saturdays and shop. Shortly after she had arrived there, she got a call from her brother, Melissa asked him if he was ready to get clean, and he was, and two weeks later, she had him in treatment.

I picked up my son and drove him to treatment, and I remember him saying that he was a bad person. I told him, "You are not a bad person. You are a good person. The drugs make you do bad things, but that doesn't make you bad." He marbled out too, and his life got better and better for him over time. Melissa continued to do well until the boyfriend got out of jail. The drugs and the crime started all over again.

I was devastated.

My sister called me to tell me that she was using drugs again. I began to sob uncontrollably. And saying over and over again, " I can't do this again, I can't!" and my sister said to me in a very soft voice, "Yes, you can, you have to." I knew I had to for my girl. "Please, dear God, give me the strength and the courage I need to get through this."

It didn't take long before the boyfriend was re-arrested. He went to jail, and Melissa was left hanging out with all the dealers and druggies. Then one day, I got a call from the police, and they told me that they had my daughter. They said that she had not done anything wrong, but they were going to send her back home to me. They also noted that her jeep was in the impound. The story they told me made my heart stop.

The police told me they'd been watching Melissa for a while. They knew she was hanging around with the wrong people. The ringleader gets girls hooked on specific drugs and sends them off to the big city to work for him. The police said they knew Melissa from before the drugs, and she was not that kind of person, so they took it upon themselves to buy her a bus ticket home. The police said they had been watching this group for some time and were trying to catch them. I was stunned and dumbfounded. But I was so grateful that they did that. Praise God for watching over her!

That afternoon I went to meet Melissa at the bus station. There she was standing with a black garbage bag; with everything she had owned in it. She was unkempt. I shook my head and couldn't believe this was my daughter, but it was. I took her home and fed her, and she went to sleep. She ate and slept for a few days. She finally had enough nourishment in her and no drugs in her system to start telling me things that happened.

She told me that she was on social assistance and had money coming in and that she would see about getting her cheques sent to my place. She had to have money to get her jeep out of the impound. That's all that was on her mind was that stupid possessed jeep.

I told her that demons possessed the jeep, and that's why it always got her into trouble.

One day, she came to pick me up with my car, and someone went through a stop sign and hit her – totaled my car off. She went through all the proper procedures for the accident. She felt so bad that it happened. "It was an accident," I said. I would get a new vehicle. Then her money came, and she was on the bus to get her jeep.

She assured me over and over again that she would be back. She let me know when she got there and got the jeep out of the impound. She was on her way back home, but she never made it back to my place. My heart sank yet again another time. When was this going to stop, and what would it take for this to stop?

CHAPTER Seven
I Looked Death in The Eye - The Deepest of My Addiction

Have you ever thought you had hit rock bottom and couldn't go any lower? Well, you can!

You know, when you think you have lost everything and everyone, where you have nothing else to lose, well, it can get darker, and you can go deeper into that hole.

I was so mad at God, blaming my life on him, always asking, "What did I do to deserve this? Why are you punishing me?" And I don't mean the life I was living. I mean the moments when I didn't have the money to buy drugs, would not have a place to stay or a bed to lay in or a shower to shower in, food to eat, I felt God was evil to me, he was not giving me anything. "What did I do to him to deserve this?"

The following year was when I bounced around from house to house, wherever I could get someone to let me stay, sleep, or shower when I needed to.

There was a time when I smoked all my dope and didn't have any money to reload and get more. And this one time, in particular, I hit up a customer that I knew had money to see if they would lend me some so, I could get back on my feet again. Of course, I would give them half to make them happy, and they said yes.

THE DARKNESS THROUGH ADDICTION

Headed to the city to load, I decided to use a different dealer, a friend of mine, or so I thought.

He was getting to our spot where we would meet his dealer, kind of in an odd area and not the usual place to pick up outside of the city. It felt strange, but I did not think anything about it. My friend asked me to get out of the truck for a second as he needed to meet his dealer alone and said he would be right back. Again, I did not think anything of it, I jumped out, and he frantically drove away. Left in the dust, I was robbed and left behind with NOTHING, now literally having NOTHING. I stood there alone, upset and scared. Again, asking God, "what did I do to deserve this?"

Addiction is a lonely and painful disease to live with, and it robs you of everything: your spirit, dignity, self-worth, and inner being. It brings heartache, hurt, and guilt. One wrong choice can change your life forever. That drug is so potent that it will take over your life. Even if you think you have control, you don't! That drug has complete control over you, and it will conquer you if you don't take action. It will take you down when you least expect it, and before you know it, you have lost everything, and that could mean your life!!

Again, in and out of having money and drugs, bouncing from place to place, whoever would help me out and lend me money or wanted to pick up, I would hook them up in exchange for drugs.

I met this couple that lives in a beautiful home outside of town, and again I am at this low point in my life, not always having money or drugs to feed my habit.

This couple seemed nice and opened their door for me to stay there under one stipulation: I sell drugs for them. That meant that I could always have drugs on hand. Jackpot! is what was going through my mind.

They had big plans to make some good money, and I was all in. It would mean I could continue to stay high and sell drugs.

I LOOKED DEATH IN THE EYE

They supplied the drugs, and I began to deliver. I continued this for several weeks, and one night I remember I decided to party, and I ended up smoking all the drugs and only having very little money in hand to give to them, scared and unsure what the outcome was going to be. But I headed back to their place, and as expected, they were very angry with me.

I had to come up with $2000 to pay for the couple of ounces of crack they gave me to sell. Obviously! – I didn't have that amount of money.

They told me to find it. "You are not leaving this place until you have paid for the drugs you smoked." Yup, they held me captive. I was scared as hell, and the thoughts going through my mind were, "if I would never get out of here, I would never see my family again. What have I done?" I was so pissed off at myself and bloody scared and nervous.

I called my dad to see if he would lend me the money. I remember that call and my dad telling me, no, I am not giving you money. I explained that I was being held, and they were not letting me go until I had them paid back. He gave in, and I got them paid back and continued to sell drugs for them.

There were many times while I was using when I witnessed other people overdosing. Watching these people do the "chicken" on the floor. I watched them either take too big of a hoot or an injection, and then they would drop to the floor, turning blue, eyes rolling into the back of their heads and sometimes going into the "chicken." I would panic inside each time this happened but knew I had to be calm to help them come around. I would run to the bathroom, get a cold cloth, place it on their forehead, talk to them calmly, and walk them through it. I was scared shitless each time this happened.

But as an addict, being so deep into my addiction, these episodes didn't even phase me because I was invisible. In the fall of 2006, I was selling drugs for someone different and staying in his holiday trailer just outside a small town. He was "looking" after me making sure I had a warm place, food to eat, and drugs to get high.

I remember, one evening, heading to the trailer to reload my drugs to supply my customers waiting to get their high.

I arrived at the trailer, it was dark outside, and I had a weird feeling in my gut, but I didn't care because I needed more drugs, so as usual, I headed there and arrived. I went inside the trailer. He was getting ready for what I needed. We exchanged, I got my drugs, and he got his money. He was just in the process of cooking up some crack, so I stuck around to have some hoots with him before I headed down the road.

I remember sitting on the couch just in front of the doorway. I heard a vehicle driving up to the trailer; being October, the leaves were all over the ground. I listened to the leaves crunching as the car pulled up.

I was not thinking anything of it. I thought it was probably someone coming to get drugs. We continued with what we were doing. I was sitting on the couch, and my dealer was standing just over by the kitchen sink. When I heard footsteps coming up to the trailer, the door swung open, and there were two individuals in the doorway with balaclavas over their heads and guns in their hands. One was pointing at me, and one was pointing at my dealer.

At this moment, I froze, thinking, "OMG! what is going on? I am going to die. Grabbing the little pillow on the couch, I curled up in a ball and put the pillow in front of me to protect myself from the gunshot. I remembered holding my breath, waiting for the bullet to hit me.

I heard this deep voice yell out, "Where are the drugs? Where is the money? Give it to me, or we will shoot you!"

My dealer said, "I don't have anything," then, before you know it, one gunshot and a big thud, the dealer hitting the floor. Another two gunshots fired, then dead silence. The only thing I could hear was my dealer gurgling on his blood, trying to breathe. I stayed curled up for what seemed to be an eternity. I sat there so scared and unsure if the killers were gone or still standing in the doorway. I waited until I finally heard the vehicle doors close, and the vehicle drove away and then slowly started to pull the pillow away and looked around.

I am seeing my dealer's body lying on the floor while he is gurgling on his blood, eyes wide open and blood coming out of his mouth and beginning to pool around his upper body. I remember saying to him, "Help will come. You're going to be okay!" Standing there shaking and scared spitless, I began to grab the drugs and money he had, together with the pipes, so that I could hide it all before the police came. I scramble to put the paraphrenia away.

The people that owned the property came out and brought me inside their house. Once inside, I ran and locked myself in the bathroom, scared to death, wondering if they were going to come back and kill me. I sat in there until the police arrived, having hoots one right after the other.

The Royal Canadian Mounted Police arrived and put me into the back of a police car. We headed down to the station for questioning, a 3-hour process. After questioning, they placed me into a hotel, with guards sitting outside my room to protect me if the killers were coming back to finish me off.

To this day, I have no idea why I am still alive but thank God for keeping me safe that evening of the murder.

The next day the police let me go, and I headed back to the place I was staying at the time, and Ahhh! that hoot was just what I needed to numb my feelings and not think about the murder.

Having some friends come to pick me up, we headed to town. I was in the back seat, feeling very uneasy and not comfortable. I was a bit off, to say the least, from my experience a few days before. And the passenger in the front seat had a gun and turned around and pointed it at me. I was terrified and had a flashback and started crying, asking him not to do that.

At the darkest time in my addiction, I knew I had nothing left in my life, pushing my family away. I knew they were done with me, my behavior, and lies. All I had left was my crack pipe and my needle in hand; that's it! My desire to live was gone. I was lost, confused, and unsure what to do with myself. My will to live was long gone.

Chapter Eight
The Valley of Death

On her way back to my place, she had decided that she would stop and see some friends after picking up her jeep. Yes, friends would help her forget all her problems by getting high. After that, she always called me and told me that she wanted to quit this, and I would say to her, "when you're sick and tired of being sick and tired, you will do something about it."

Now that the boyfriend was in jail, for who knows how long, she just hung around all of their old bad friends doing drugs and selling them. That was how she was making money.

Since Melissa had had an accident with my car and it was totaled, and the insurance company took forever to pay out my insurance, I decided to take the bus to see my parents since it was Mother's Day. That was a long trip to the next province to see them, and it also would give me a chance to regroup and recharge.

My mom was always my go-to person. If it wasn't for her, I don't know how I could have gotten through many things. She always gave the best advice and always cheered me on. We had a great visit. Then on Sunday morning, I heard on the radio about an accident that happened on one of the highways close by, and a child died, and I said to my mom, that would be just horrible to have that happen on Mother's Day.

Then about an hour after we had had supper, I got a phone call from my youngest daughter who told me that she had gone over to my place and just after she got in the door the phone rang and she answered it. It was a police officer, and he asked her if she knew Melissa, and she told him that she was her sister and that I was away.

The officer told my youngest daughter about Melissa being in an accident. He said Melissa got sent to the hospital and had a breathing tube. Although my youngest daughter didn't, I knew what that meant, and right then, I was glad she didn't know. I didn't want her to drive like a crazy man to the hospital.

She told them that she would get a hold of me and tell me what happened. My youngest daughter had called, and I got off the phone with her, and I was hysterical. I didn't know what to do. I didn't have a car, so I couldn't just jump in it and go. I just was lost, and my mind wouldn't work. My dad had suggested that I take a plane and fly there. But I said it could be tomorrow before I get there. It could be too late.

My parents suggested that I call my brother-in-law. He said he would make some phone calls. About 15 minutes later, he called back and told me to get ready to go. He had called his job, got time off, and drove me to the hospital. We drove in almost complete silence. My mind was going around and around. Tears would run down my face, and I felt short of breath at times. I wondered if she would still be alive when I got there.

I felt like I could run faster than the car was going, but we had done it in four and a half hours when we got to the hospital. It was usually a six-hour drive from where I was, but it took us only four and a half hours. I guess we were flying. My youngest daughter and her brother met me at the doors when we arrived. They told me what was going on and that I should call in to see her. So I called and went in. My brother-in-law came in with me to have some support and have a shoulder to cry on if I needed it, and man, man, I needed that shoulder. As I stood by Melissa's bed, she turned her head, looked up at me, and said around the breathing tube.

"Mom, I love you," and I said, "I love you back." She was bruised up and had lacerations on her hands and arms. She also had a collar on because she had a head and neck injury, and she was so thin. She had tubes and lines coming from so many places on her body. My brother-in-law was also in shock because of all the tubes and life support apparatus.

The tears were streaming down my face. The doctors said they wanted to talk to the family the following day. I didn't sleep much. I knew how things went in ICU, and I wasn't looking forward to the talk.

My son, my youngest daughter, Melissa's dad, his wife, my brother-in-law, and I were all in the room for the update. The doctors had decided they would pull the breathing tube to see how she would do and do many tests to see how bad the brain damage was.

Melissa had had a brain trauma in the accident. She had no major broken bones, only broken ribs, which caused a need for a chest tube. Pulling the breathing tube went well, and they took her to a unit. The doctors asked Melissa to do different things, like touching her toes, and she did not know what they were asking. She had no idea what they had asked her to do.

I turned around and walked into the bathroom, and cried ever so hard. My youngest daughter came in and hugged me and tried consoling me but couldn't. I needed the time to release the emotions that I had built up.

My daughter and I would help with Melissa's care for the following days. We would give her a bed bath and change her gown. There was nothing left but skin and bones. Her skin was an ashen color, and her hands were black stained from smoking drugs.

THE DARKNESS THROUGH ADDICTION

Melissa couldn't even talk a single word – it was like her brain was jumbled up. She could not follow a simple command, but she was mean. She would pinch you if you tried rubbing her arm.

The nurses put on five-point restraints to work with her and provide her care. It wasn't pleasant to see. Her personality had changed, and she would easily get angry. She had to use a walker to walk and had lots of therapy to help heal her brain. She was in the hospital for a long time. Melissa and her ex-husband had remained friends, and he came along with me quite a few times to see her. It was nice to have company for the drive there.

Then one day, when my youngest daughter and I were leaving the hospital, we spotted Melissa's jeep. Her so-called friends were using it for who knows what. I also didn't want them going to see Melissa. So, my youngest daughter and I went back to the unit in the hospital and told the nurses that no one was to see her—only family. We had to use a password to get in to see her. A few weeks after the accident and with therapy, Melissa started talking again and making sense.

I had to go back to work long before Melissa was released. I had lots of healing to do also with the accident. I was a broken mess. I had no idea how I would get through all of this. I hated my life. I was barely making a living. I lived in a tiny one-bedroom basement apartment and an old car and owed lots of money.

Then one day, when I was walking to work, I remembered a bible verse that said, "Be ye grateful in and for all things." I couldn't believe it. God wanted me to be grateful for what, this accident? And it also doesn't say if you feel like it; it says to be thankful. So, I started walking and thanking God for everything I was grateful for. Then, a few small things became more important things. I began to feel better about life. I had joy in my soul again.

One day at work, I happened to turn around, and the charge nurse, who was a good friend of mine, was sitting staring at me,

THE VALLEY OF DEATH

and she said to me, "how do you do it? It's no wonder your kids call you their rock". I asked, "how do I do what?" How have you not fallen apart in all of this." I sat there and said in a calm voice. "Grace, God's Grace. I could have never gotten through this if it wasn't for God's help."

The unit that I worked on weren't just friends. They had become my family, and to my surprise, one day, they had all gotten together and put money in an envelope for me to help with expenses. It cost a lot of money to drive back and forth to see Melissa while in the hospital.

I could not believe how much they gave me.

It was, indeed, a miracle.

There was enough in there for all the expenses I had from driving back and forth to see Melissa. Then the day came that she needed to go home. Was this time going to be different? Melissa had told me that she was given a second chance in life.

After Melissa got out of the hospital, the following days were challenging for sure. There were problems, but we overcame them together. The old crowd hanging around before the accident somehow found out that she was out of the hospital and wanted to connect with her.

I did my best to stop it. The guy that was driving her jeep the day we saw it at the hospital ended up getting arrested in it, and he went to jail for some crimes that he had done, and the Jeep was impounded again. The guy in prison somehow got a message and wanted to talk to her.

She had talked to him in jail, and he wanted her to visit and call him in prison. But with no money, that was hard to do, and with the "Mom's bank" being broke, even harder. So that was over quickly.

Then we took a drive and got the jeep out of the impound. But it sat still for quite some time in my driveway. She was terrified to drive. Also, her memory was not good. I would take her shopping. I would tell her to get the things she needed. She would go but come back in a few minutes and asked again what she needed. I would tell her, and she would go again looking for what she needed. It took quite a long time for her memory to improve, but it did.

Then one day, I suggested we see her grandparents. She loved them and thought a lot of their advice. I had told her that she was going to drive there. She needed to overcome the fear of driving. She did well but would not pass anyone on the highway. But that was alright – It was a start.

While we were there, she met a nice guy, and the two of them hit it off. They spent lots of time together while we were visiting my parents. I had told her that she could have a nice guy. They talked on the phone for a while but realized that this relationship was too complicated. It was too far away. But it gave her confidence that she could maybe have someone good.

Shortly after we got home from our visit to her grandparents' place, she asked if I would take her to see the car she was in the accident. So, we went to the police station to find out where it was. She also had charges laid against her that day too. She talked to the officer that was on that day of the accident. She had no recollection of the accident at all. She had so many questions as she didn't remember anything from before, during, and after the accident.

The officer had told her that he had just started working there and it was his first accident that he had to go to. He said to her that he would never forget her screaming. He said that they didn't expect her to live or make a recovery. Some of the nurses I worked with had told her that sometimes the brain won't remember. It's the brain's way of protecting you.

The officer told her where the car was, so Melissa and I went to see it. I was horrified, and so was she. The vehicle had split in two. The back seat and trunk of the car were in a ball, and the front was crushed. "How did she survive?"

She told me that day that there was someone in the back seat, and she wondered where they were and what had happened to them. There had been nobody in the back seat, but I looked at her and said, "Yes, there was. Your guardian angel was there with you to protect you." She was alive by the grace of God, and I was thankful.

She kept telling me that she should go back to treatment. So she tried to get government assistance to go, but there was no help, and the only available treatment center was all women. Melissa always had a hard time talking with women. Maybe it was because she was always around boys when she was little.

She was always with her brothers and their friends. She always was a bit of a tomboy.

We talked about it, and I said maybe it would be good for her to go with all women to learn something from them. Next was the money part, but the staff had given me enough money to pay my expenses, plus there was enough for treatment. So, she went.

She did learn a lot, and she was ready. The lady councilor that was there was just what she needed. Not that it was easy when she came out. It was not. There were lots of big bumps and temptations along the way

CHAPTER Nine
The Death Bed

The phone was ringing, and nobody was answering on the other end as I was trying to call my mom. I was calling to tell her that I was sick and tired of living this life, and I wanted help. With nobody answering, I left that exact message.

But not even knowing what was around the corner for me.

On Mother's Day of 2008, I was getting ready to head into the city to pick up my drugs. I'd called and made arrangements to meet with my dealer. I was excited, as I usually was, because at this time, I was getting low on my supply, and I needed my drugs to live and survive.

I stopped to pick up an acquaintance, one of my customers that wanted to come along for the ride. And we headed into the city in a white Cadillac that one of my customers lent to me. I was paying him with drugs.

I am about to tell you what information was said to me by the RCMP because I don't remember a single thing from this event. I have no memory of a week after.

On my way to meet my dealer, I was headed west down the highway. I was approaching a vehicle on the road, and I proceeded to pass, but there was an oncoming vehicle as I was passing the other car. I attempted to hit the brakes and get back into my lane, where I lost control and collided with the oncoming vehicle.

From the evidence I saw and what I was told, my car split in half. The vehicle's front ended on the north side of the highway, and the rear on the south side of the road another 30 feet away. The paramedics found me still sitting in the driver's seat, but my passenger had flown into the field.

Star Air Ambulance responded to the scene and evacuated me because my condition was critical. They intubated me at the accident scene and airlifted me to the hospital.

I was in rough shape. I was placed on life support and had three tubes placed into my lungs to drain them. Because my ribs were broken, they punctured my lungs and caused hemopneumothorax. They didn't think I was going to make the night.

The police tried to contact my mom at her house, but she was not home. My younger sister answered the phone to hear the terrible news. She got a hold of my mom, who was out of province at my grandparents'.

In a panic, because of the state I was in and hearing from the doctors that I would not make it that night, she and my uncle got into the car and drove at high speeds to get to me in time before I was gone.

After being on life support and in the ICU department for over a week, they moved me to the other side. Here is when I can begin to remember things; waking up and not knowing what was happening around me; I was confused.

As I lay propped up in my bed, looking around, it was bright out. Mid-day, I remember looking over to my left towards the door and seeing a lady (not sure who she was), my oldest brother, and my dad walking through the door. I remember they all had smiles on their faces, but I was still confused about where I was and what was going on.

THE DEATH BED

I had these tubes coming out of my chest, one on the side, one on the upper back, and one on the mid-back. These tubes led to large cases with what looked like tar inside them. These machines cleared my pleural space because my broken ribs punctured my lung in the accident.

As the days passed and my visitors came and went, things started to set in, my mind became clear, and I remember my mom and I were talking. She told me what happened, that I was in a bad car accident, was airlifted, and on life support for three days. They didn't think I was going to make the night.

The police called me while I was in the hospital to break the news.

"You're going to charge me with what?!"

My heart sank in my chest! "Was this happening to me?"

What am I going to do?

What will my mom think?

What will my family think?

I had to use a walker to walk for most of my time there, as I had fractured my tailbone, and my entire body was in pain. I remember standing up on both feet, and it hurt to put one foot in front of the other. The walker helped me walk, but it also carried my "suitcases'' around, LOL. That's what I called the things attached to my lungs. I began physical therapy and speech therapy to help me talk and communicate again. I hoped it would allow me to communicate better with others.

My mom was there by my side the whole time. She was always there to comfort me regardless of what I'd put her throught in the past. She was there, and she loved me. If it was not for her, I don't know how I would have gotten through these days in the hospital. I looked forward to every day because I knew that she would be coming by to see me and brighten my day. She gave me hope.

THE DARKNESS THROUGH ADDICTION

Although I was alone in my hospital bed, sad and depressed, I thought about all I did to myself, my family, and others – I was heartbroken. I had an enormous amount of guilt for what I had done and where it led me in my life. I remember how my heart was heavy and dark, often crying myself to sleep and just wanting to die. I knew this was it, that I had to change my habits and get clean.

The nurses and doctors always kept saying to me how lucky I was.

The last chest tube was removed as days passed, and it was almost time to go home. I was so ready and excited but also scared!!

I knew what this could mean, potentially going back down my dark path. The path that I seemed to go down when I got another chance. But this time was different. I did a lot of thinking and saw what happened due to my drug use. I didn't want to go down that dark path. I desired to turn things around, but I was deathly scared to leave, not knowing if I would have the willpower or strength to stay clean.

On the day I was discharged from the hospital, I had many emotions. I was excited to be out (a month was way too long to be in the hospital), but I was anxious to go because I was in a safe place where I knew I could not go back to drugs, I was afraid because I was not sure if I was going to relapse. But I had to face my fear and emotions in my head and heart and got into the vehicle.

I had no other option, and mom would not let me go. So I slowly got myself into the backseat. It took all I had, and my body was still in so much pain from my injuries. I lay down in the back seat. Mom had to pull over about halfway because my body needed to stretch. I was in an unbearable amount of pain throughout my whole body.

THE DEATH BED

Back at mom's place, feeling safe and supported by her. I knew deep in my heart and soul that this was my time. I had to clean up this time as I may not get another chance next time.

Crazy, out of all the things I went through on my journey, it took me almost losing my life, being on my deathbed, finally waking up, and wanting to become clean. Drugs were not an option. I knew I had to be strong, focused, committed, and determined to overcome this.

I am and will forever be grateful for the wonderful people who were there for my mom, the unit where she worked, and all the people that supported and fundraiser for her. Your actions allowed my mom to take time off to be by my side when I needed her the most. And with the remainder of the funds, mom was kind enough to pay for me to get into treatment. Thank you so much, Mom! from the bottom of my heart, this is what changed my life forever. I was open and ready for this next chapter in my life.

Chapter Ten
The Change

*"Tell them how much the Lord has done for you,
and how he has mercy on you."*
(Mark 5:19 - NIV)

Melissa stayed with me for a while after treatment. She would visit people that she used to know from her old life. She would talk to them about how she felt and getting a second chance. They all looked up to her for getting clean. And for me, when she left to visit, these people would put me on edge. I was always wondering if she would come home. Her sister would come over a lot after she came out of treatment. It was so good to see the two of them together.

They were always each other's best friends. After Melissa was well enough, she found a job with a law firm.

The lawyer who hired her knew all about her but said everyone deserves a second chance. Once she started working and making money, she got herself a place to live. Her sister became one of her roommates for a while.

She was tempted to go back to the drug world, but she said she would play the tape in her head. She also went to meetings where she could talk to other recovering addicts. This was so good for her to connect with others like her. They would help each other.

There was a time that she was out walking at lunchtime. That was something she did every day. Melissa loves to exercise. As she was walking, she noticed a bag of cocaine lying on the sidewalk.

She stood and looked at it but didn't pick it up. As soon as she got back to the office, she phoned me and told me what had happened. She was so proud that she had just left it there. I, too, was very proud of her. Many temptations like this happened to her, but she remained steady. She said she was given a second chance, and she has always wanted to help people that have an addiction problem like her. She has always said if she can do it, anyone can do it.

After about a year after the accident, Melissa and her brother got a place together. One day, her brother and a guy he worked with and I went out for breakfast with Melissa. The guy her brother worked with asked her brother if he could date his sister.

Melissa and this new guy hit it off. They were always together, and before long, the two of them moved in together. Shortly after Melissa had gotten out of treatment, I had asked why she always was with these loser guys. She deserved better than that and that she should write exactly what she wanted in a guy on a piece of paper. So she did. Shortly after they moved in together, I gave her the paperback on which she wrote the description – he was exactly what she had written down on this paper.

When Melissa was a teenager, she was told that she would never conceive a child. The one thing Melissa wanted more than anything was to be a mother. So, she and her future husband started the procedure of IVF.

The first attempt did not work, and Melissa was devastated, but the second time worked, and they had a baby boy. The following year, she was married to the guy of her dreams and had another baby boy a year later.

THE CHANGE

Melissa's happily ever after finally happened for her.

It was a long journey to get there, but she made it. She continues to use what she learned in treatment, and with the fantastic support of her husband and her family, she continues to do well. Her heart was always and remains to help someone with addictions and find the best in yourself.

When Melissa was clean for ten years, she could go back to the treatment center that she had attended and receive her medallion. She got up in front of all the people at the treatment center and shared her journey with them. She inspired a lot of them. I was very proud of listening to her speak.

The one thing that Melissa and I had before and while she got into drugs was that she always came to me to talk. It was as if she needed me or be close to me or hear my voice. It always seemed like Melissa had to learn life lessons the hard way. She would listen to advise but didn't always take the advice. She was stubborn, which she has learned to use for her good. Specially to follow a better road in life and chase her dreams.

The months and years we have had after the accident has been the best. I have been and always will be her best friend. Even though the drugs, I was her go-to person. I was her rock and her constant. The one that was always there no matter what. She always comes to me in the sad and hard times and the happy times. I was with her through her wedding and pregnancies and the joy of seeing her sons grow.

One of her sons was diagnosed with diabetes. He was only 18 months old. Melissa cried so hard when she found this out. She said she would never learn it all. But Melissa and her husband went to work and learned it all. It is so amazing watching the two of them figure out his carbs and insulin. A year after his diagnosis, they could put together a meal, and they knew exactly how many carbs were in that dish. I was so amazed. When Melissa needs to learn something, she puts her whole heart into it. I also remember a time that her younger sister needed help.

Melissa went right to work and had support for her around the clock.

We enjoy times at my summer place where the boys come out to ride in the cart. Every Christmas eve, we are together. We have appetizers, and then Melissa's husband tours Melissa, the boys, and me around town, looking at all the lights. Memories through the eyes of a child.

As a whole family, we all love our time together and love each other immensely. We have a love for each other that is unconditional. It doesn't mean we all agree about everything, but we are all there for each other in the good times and the hard times. There is a special kind of bond our family has, and it brings my heart joy.

I am so proud of who Melissa has become. And I am proud to call myself Mom to every one of my children. They are just what I need. The one thing we all do is hug each other before we leave each other. I want them to know that I always will love them.

If I couldn't have drawn strength and courage from God, I would have never gotten through these trials. But here I am with all my family, and I am so very proud of every one of them.

Chapter Eleven
My Next Chapter in Life: "You're Always One Decision Away from A Totally Different Life."

I had asked myself many times why God saved my life and let me live through everything I was faced with on this dark journey.

After my accident, my mom would always say to me, "God has a plan for you Melissa, you are here for a reason."

After all that I had been through, I truly felt he did have a plan, but what was it? I kept asking myself and kept searching for an answer.

As I sit here today, I am so grateful for my heavenly Father, who watched over me each day on my journey of darkness. He knew what I had to go through so that one day I could impact the lives of many.

You know they say the stubborn ones will reach their desired goals in life and overcome anything that gets in their way. They will not give up until they have accomplished what they have set out to do.

That was me; after that accident, I knew it was my time to shine, but to shine, I needed to change. Change is hard, discomforting, painful, and challenging, but change can be a beautiful process, and the outcome is rewarding.

THE DARKNESS THROUGH ADDICTION

I knew I had a long road ahead of me and was going to face many challenges, but I knew I had to commit to myself, to this process, and ask God for guidance.

If you ask anyone who knows me, they will tell you that I will conquer it when I commit and put my energy into something.

And that was what I did!!!

A few years after my accident, I met the man of my dreams, the one I have always been searching for but never found until he crossed my path at the divine time. He was a kind and gentle soul with a heart of gold, and we fell in love instantly.

I always wanted to have kids but was told at a young age that I would never be able to, so we looked into the process of IVF. It was a considerable investment, but this was something that both of us wanted, so we sold some things and made it happen.

So, we began the process. I was thrilled, just like a little girl at a candy store. Finally, my dream was going to come true, becoming a mother. The process took a good 4-5 months, but we were eager and ready.

The final step in the process came to implant the egg. I remember it fell on the weekend of my sisters' stagette party, thank goodness it was a Sunday so that I could attend and celebrate with her. I got my last medication late Saturday evening, and off to bed, I went.

Up early, mom and I headed off to the hospital for the big day. OMG, I was so excited and nervous at the same time. I lay on my bed, waiting for the nurses to come to get us to take us into the room for the procedure. I remember looking over at my husband and looking into his eyes. Seeing the excitement within him was magical. We were about to become parents.

It was such an extraordinary experience to watch; laying there, I am not going to lie, I was terrified inside, just not knowing what to expect with the procedure. Will it hurt? Will it not hurt? My palms were sweaty, and my heart was going a mile a minute. Then, the doctor arrived in the room to start.

First, calling out our names and asking us to look up at the screen, there it was, our egg magnified so we could see it. We had to confirm the name underneath it, and away they went. Inserting a catheter into my uterus, the doctor said, "Okay, let's do this!" We sat there and watched the egg (which looked like a tiny bubble in the tube) go through the catheter and get to its final destination, where they implanted it, and it was complete.

Now it was just a matter of time before we found out that am were pregnant. Getting home and taking it easy, I didn't want to mess this up. I am afraid I will lose the egg if I moved too much or the wrong way. It was a long ten days, to say the least.

After the long wait, day 10 arrived, and we went in for blood work, still having to wait another day or two before the doctor called us with the results.

The clinic called me while I was at work, and I called back on my first break. "Melissa, I am sorry to tell you, but the result came back negative you are not pregnant. We can try again in a few months." My heart dropped, and I began to cry.

I sat there in silence, crying, knowing I could not be at work right then, so I asked the manager if I could leave, and she agreed. I called my husband, and we cried together on the phone.

I would ask God, "Why me? Why are you doing this to me? I am doing good in my life at last! I am clean and creating a better life for myself."

I was in such a wrong place after finding out this news. You see, I was clean but never worked on bettering myself. I lived in a negative mindset, had tons of negative self-talk, lived with guilt and shame from my past.

THE DARKNESS THROUGH ADDICTION

A few months went by, and we tried a second time, and it was successful. I was pregnant!! And eight months later, we were blessed with our first son.

Becoming a parent was the best gift I could ever receive. I was so thankful for such a healthy, beautiful boy. Giving birth and holding my son, looking into his eyes, was the most magical experience. I was on cloud nine and didn't want that moment to end. After holding him for a few minutes, the nurses had to take him to ICU because he was a month early. He stayed in ICU for 13 days, and we got a place at the Ronald McDonald House so that we could be close to our son and see him every second that we could.

As happy and excited as I was, there was a part of me that went into that negative self-talk. I was asking God again, "Why me? Why are you doing this to me? I don't deserve this."

Or do I?? Maybe this is God's way of punishing me for what I had done in my past. The negativity was always showing up in my life.

They say if you live in a negative mindset, you will attract negativity, and that was me. Just because I was clean and living a good life didn't mean I had it all together because I didn't.

My husband and I decided our son needed a brother or sister as time went on. So we contacted the doctors and started the process. Twelve months later, in 2013, we were blessed with our second baby boy, healthy and beautiful.

Our life was now complete, and I am forever grateful.

While on maternity leave with my second son, I loved every aspect of being a mom and being with them every day. I knew in my heart that I didn't want to return to work full time or at all, for that matter.

This is when Network Marketing fell into my lap, and my prayers got answered. I have seen the vision and committed myself to the process. Dove in with both feet and ranked up fast to leadership. I was bringing in some good cash. Enough that when my maternity leave was over, I could return to work only two days a week. I felt so blessed because that meant more time with my boys. A few years later, I retired from the legal assistant career.

With Network Marketing came a lot of self-development. I wanted to take it to another level and was ready too because I still found myself falling back into a negative state if something was not going in the right direction. But I knew I could not do it on my own, and let's face it, and I didn't have my shit together. I had so much negative self-talk and lived in a negative mindset. And I needed to get out of it if I wanted to become that Leader and Mentor that I was inside my soul.

I Invested in myself and dove into Bob Proctor's program Thinking into Results with my mentor, Myla. She worked closely with me, and things began to shift now.

I began to work on my mindset to learn how to shift it when negative things were happening around me. I began to work on my limiting beliefs, writing them out and replacing them with positive ones. I worked on my paradigms, one by one, taking the paradigm that kept me stuck and replacing it with a new one, repeating it over and over until it became a habit. Writing my "I am" statements, I began to believe them over time.

I continued my journey with my business, but I hit a wall after a few years. It began to go downhill. I was losing my team and unable to bring anyone else on because I ran out of my warm market and didn't have the right skill sets. I began to repel people away because of the strategies used on my social media.

Feeling defeated and fearing to go back to my corporate job, I began to search for other ways to grow my business. I invested in a program that taught me how to level up my business and attract people.

In the community within this program, I met some incredible mentors. I began to follow them and saw their success in their own Network Marketing businesses; I was amazed. It was a no-brainer to me, and I locked arms with them.

If it were not for their mentorship, knowledge, and roadmap, I would not be where I am today in my business, living the life of freedom and choices.

Since becoming an entrepreneur and dropping into my true passion of helping others, watching others grow, and being that leader and mentor to guide them through the ups and downs, I knew I was on the right path to finding my whole purpose in life. I was getting closer to what it was that God had planned for me. I felt it in my heart.

What got the thoughts going was when I attended the treatment center to get my 10-year medallion in 2017, there I was standing and sharing my story in a room full of addicts in treatment. My story touched everyone there, and they began to ask questions. I stood up there for an hour, helping and encouraging these people that there is hope. It felt pretty magical.

When I was in treatment myself, and someone received their medallion, I said to myself, "Soon, that it will be me!"

What got me excited was a gentleman in treatment who shared with me, he said "Do you remember this board?" (it was a board where every morning in a group session, you would share with the group where you were on a scale of 1-10)."Well, when I first started my day, I was at a 0 but listening to your story and your inspiration to live life, I am now at a 10."

WOW!! That made my day; I inspired someone so much!

I left there on fire. I felt so amazing that I had impacted so many people in that treatment center, and that's when I knew what my purpose was: to inspire, motivate, and help others overcome the obstacles they faced in their lives. But I didn't know how I was going to make this happen. Always on my mind, I continued to search and pray that God would direct me in the right direction.

It wasn't until about a year ago, after 12 years when I accepted that I was a recovering drug addict and was okay with that. I used to be so ashamed of being an addict that I kept it a deep dark secret. I would not tell anyone. I was too embarrassed to share because I was fearful of judgment. I felt that they would label me and think of me differently because of who I used to be.

But over time, I began to tap into myself and work on things.

Becoming content with myself and accepting it has allowed me to be vulnerable in my life, and for that, I have truly stepped into myself, which allowed me to heal from my past and my decisions. My body, mind, and soul are in alignment with each other.

In January 2021, I was presented with a pretty incredible opportunity to become a sales coach and help other network markets learn magnetic marketing and gain traction in their business.

Again, I invested in myself for growth and new skillsets, joined SOS Academy, and fully committed myself to the process. One week in, I was placed on a sales team and committed myself to the team's journey. After a month in, I hit the top coach and have maintained this for the entire year, and in fact, I still am the leading sales coach.

Life was amazing and going in the right direction. My businesses were thriving, and we were doing great financially. I was doing what I loved to do, helping others and changing lives worldwide.

Shortly after starting my sales coaching, I was introduced to hypnotherapy through my mentorship within the coaching. I began sessions with a hypnotherapist, Charlotte Chalkley. Thank you so much, Charlotte; you are a true blessing. These sessions blew my mind away, so much shifted within me. I was becoming clearer in all areas of my life.

After a few sessions, I discovered that my passion for helping others was hypnotherapy. I saw the changes emerge within myself in a short time. I knew I could help others turn their lives around using this method.

I was amazed by my transformation and wanted to learn hypnotherapy to help others in their lives.

I began to love myself again, which I can't remember the last time I did. I was able to forgive myself and others from my past. I could work through some of the darkest memories I was faced with on my journey. And with that, I have been able to heal my soul and become clear of my process. The calmness that has happened within is breathtaking. I am at peace with myself, which was the #1 goal when I started. Pretty cool, right?!

I have found myself. I live my life with an open and heart full of gratitude, with a positive mindset that radiates from within me to those I encounter.

I am living my best life clean and sober.

Continuing to work on me daily has allowed me to step into my full potential and create a life for my family. I continue to keep showing up for myself every single day. I wake up with a heart full of gratitude and end my day with a heart full of gratitude. I journal the moment my eyes open, and journal before my eyes close. Asking myself, "what am I grateful for" and writing out 4-5 things and reading them back to me, feeling them in my heart.

When negative things happen, I remind myself that it's Satan trying to bring me down, and I observe the situation immediately and take the positive out. For example, my day is booked with coaching clients, and one does not show up. They didn't message me to let me know. Before, I would be so pissed off, start that negative self-talk, and beat myself up. Now, I take the positive and say to myself, "Okay, awesome." I have some extra time now to catch up on calls or messages or spend time with my boys.

I continue to have my hypnotherapy sessions to help me work more around my subconscious mind. I have discovered the deep-rooted beliefs that have become a part of who I am to help resolve the traumas and things that don't serve me anymore in my life today.

I take my health very seriously. I watch what I put into my body. I am constantly improving at the gym and doing any physical activity, whether by teaching B Class, taking a spin class, walking, or running.

I am truly living my dream life. You know, the fairytale life I dreamt about when I was a child? I am living that today!!! I am truly blessed.

I am a successful 6-figure entrepreneur, coach, and hypnotherapist, helping individuals tap into their potential, help with goal setting, and help them work on their skills. I help people remove their negative self-talk, limiting beliefs, and ultimately shift their mindset to live and build their best lives and dreams in just a way that is right for them.

I get to work for myself and build my dreams which allows us to say YES to opportunities for our boys and give them the life they deserve with adventure and experiences. We can just pick up and do things at the drop of a dime. We love to spend time with our family and friends, go camping, side-by-siding, sledding, Skidoo, and travel. We are an adventurous family.

Purchasing our dream home, a month ago has brought joy and peace to our family. I still sit here in an aww. Looking around and saying to my husband daily, "Wow, hun, look what we have, this is ours. I love this place so much."

Sitting there in the lawyer's office signing the papers, I reflected over the year on how far I have come and what I have genuinely been able to create for my family. I was so proud of myself. My hard work, perseverance, dedication, and mindset to never give up have paid off!! Wow! What an incredible feeling to know where I once was. I was at the bottom, near-death, and now, look where I am, thriving and at the top!

And to top that off, I recently took on a bikini competition, an 18-week journey to improve myself on a deeper level and push myself to new limits.

During this journey, it was a time for growth, growth on a spiritual level, growth on a physical level, and growth on an emotional level. I was tying everything together with my life.

Through hypnotherapy, I worked on myself at a deeper level. I connected with my soul, which has allowed me to walk with my fears and conquer anything on my path. I overcame something that I had wanted to do for a long time, and my self-consciousness held me back for years. I placed 3rd place in open, 3rd place in true novice, and 4th in matters 35+.

Continuing with this fitness lifestyle, I will compete again in 2022.

This beautiful thing called life is precious and abundant in all aspects. I can genuinely say that I have connected my body, mind, and soul, and the energies within are aligned.

I found that my true purpose in life, alongside helping others, was to share my darkest memories and experiences with you, hoping that I would help YOU or someone around you overcome their darkest moments. To help, you can rise above them and overcome whatever it is in life that stops you from fulfilling your purpose so that you can unleash that inner spark inside your soul.

I am not sharing my story of addiction and struggle to impress you, but to impress upon you that you can do this too!!

Whatever you are going through in life, you will get through it, I promise. IF I CAN DO IT, SO CAN YOU!

MY NEXT CHAPTER IN LIFE

It doesn't matter what your story is or was. It does not matter your past, where you came from, or what you did. You can change the direction and rewrite your story right now, right here.

Don't let Satan take over, shift that mindset, get out of the negative, surround yourself with people you want to be like, people who will be there for you, people who will push you, people who lift you. Start working on yourself because you are worth it. You have so much to give; it's your turn to step into it.

Throw that negative self-talk in the garbage. You are unique in your way. You have your talents and potential needed to be seen.

YOU are enough!

YOU are worthy!

YOU are beautiful!

YOU are smart!

YOU are a leader!

YOU are amazing!

So, wherever you are, I want you to know that you have a spark within you that needs to be seen, that needs to be heard, that needs to be lightened. Open your heart and allow it to shine, and it will enable that spark within you to shine.

It's okay to admit that you need help and that you're struggling. There is help out there waiting for you. You have to put your hand out to receive. Yup, there is fear inside you, but I want you to step back and acknowledge that fear. See your fear, know it's there, observe that fear, and then I walk with that fear, side by side. Don't force it. Allow it to be there with you.

You got this!!!

Chapter Twelve
My Letter to You

To that 12-year-old reading this,

You, who is struggling right now, I was there, and I know what you're going through exactly.

The feeling of not having that parent present, the sense of abandonment, loneliness, not being good enough, not worthy enough, not smart enough, or pretty enough. I know all that negative self-talk that is going on in your head right now. I know it's shitty, I know it's dark, I know it's lonely, I know you want to run and hide from it, I know you want to numb it so you don't have to deal with it or feel it. I get it; I was there.

When you don't have that father figure in your life, all you want is to be loved, seen, and heard, and you're not getting it. You want it so bad. You cry yourself to sleep at night because you're so lonely. You miss him so bad. All you want is to be loved. You crave it so bad that you begin to lash out to search for it. You begin to seek it, and then one day it's there, you think your dreams are being answered, and a man has fallen into your life.

A MAN, how disgusting is that someone nine years older than you. Who in their right mind would seek out a 12-year-old girl?

THE DARKNESS THROUGH ADDICTION

He will comfort you, get close to you, take your virginity away, make you feel loved, and stick a needle in your arm. You have let someone take full advantage of you, and you've been blindsided. You are this innocent little child whose life is about to be destroyed.

You rebel towards your mom because you're so mad at her, and you blame her for all this. You think your dad is not around because she left and tore the family apart. Why would you want to listen to her? All you can think of is hurting you as she hurt you.

I want you to know that there is more to life than running from this feeling and the pain you are suffering. You are loved, beautiful, and on this earth for a reason.

To that 24-year-old reading this,

Who is trying to get clean right now? I was there with you, and I know what you're going through exactly.

You're in a nightmare, and you can't wake up.

The feeling of anxiety is setting in. Getting clean scares you because it's out of your comfort zone. You don't know what it's like to be "normal" because your normal is high and sketched out. You're afraid of what is ahead.

Your mind keeps going back and forth, you want to get clean because you know you're killing yourself, you feel like death, and you know it's the right thing to do, but that voice inside your head, "Satan" is telling you differently and feeding your head with negativity.

You have hit rock bottom, lost everything, and lost your family and their trust. You have lost yourself and have nothing to show but a black garbage bag full of stolen clothes. There is no roof over your head, not a penny in your pocket. Your pipe burnt from you hitting it in hopes of getting that rush. You're sketching the floor and your pockets in hopes that there is just one more hit in there.

You're crying because all you want is another hit, just one more. "Please God, give me one more, then I will get clean, I promise."

You're at the point where you need to steal to support your habit, and you're stealing from innocent people and your own family.

Maybe your next step is to sell your body, give someone a blow job or have sex with them in exchange for a hoot.

This dark hole keeps getting darker, and you keep getting further into the hole. There is no light at the end of the whole. You're lost and confused and not knowing where to go or what to do with yourself.

You have NOTHING left, feeling hopeless!!

WHAT IF

You take your next hit, which is your last hit,

WHAT IF

What if you don't make it out alive? What if you die,

THEN WHAT???

That drug has taken over you and conquered you.

THE DARKNESS THROUGH ADDICTION

The clock can't move fast enough. You want the days to end so you can circle up in bed and sleep. You look like shit, you're skinny, haven't washed your hair for days, you feel dirty, and you don't feel good in your skin.

You're feeling like shit, no energy, you are so weak because your body is going through withdrawals, shaking, sweating, and moody AF. You're pacing back and forth, not knowing what to think or do with yourself. You want the day to end, the nightmare to be over, the shakes to be gone, the sweat to stop.

The feelings of shame and guilt begin to set in, and all you can think about is a hit so that you can have that feeling of numbness, so you don't have to feel this way.

It's so hard to be clean. It's so hard to deal with life and to deal with those feelings that you are so used to running and hiding.

As you sit there in silence, your heart is racing, and all you can think of is that hit that will make you invincible. I hear you; it fucking sucks when you can't have that hit, and you want it so badly. All you want to do is cry or maybe even scream. I know because I cried myself to sleep many nights and did a lot of screaming.

It's okay; let those tears fall, let those screams out. It is the beginning of a process of healing, healing your soul, letting go, and being in this moment. It's okay. I am here with you.

Let the feelings happen, don't run from them, don't force them either. Just allow them to be there and feel them. It's okay, and you're going to be okay. I PROMISE!

Take one day at a time, take 1 minute at a time, take 1 second at a time, it is okay, breath, you got this.

I want to share with you, which has helped me, and I learned this when I was in treatment: play the tape. When you feel that you want to have that hit, sit down, slow down, take some deep breaths, in through the nose and out through the mouth, allowing your breath to be in rhythm in just the way it is meant to be—slowing things down, right here, right now. Breathing in that calm and breathing out that tension, allowing your lungs to fill up with every breath and now begin to play that tape in your mind.

You go to pick up that crack hit, that needle, that bottle of booze, whatever it is that you're addicted to, and you inhale, inject or swallow that drug, you get high. Now think about that one hoot or drink, "What would be the outcome?" Perhaps you will need more and more and more. Think about what it will do to you and how it will impact you. Think of all the dark and horrible days you have gone through.

Everything that you once lost, think about losing it all over again: your parents, siblings, family, friends, loved ones, and kids. How would of feel about hurting them or losing them again? How would it feel to lose yourself again, to lose your soul, your dignity? And who knows, this time could be your last time. You may not get a second chance.

For me, if I were to pick up, I would go right back to where I was in 2008, back to weighing 90 lbs. soaking wet, looking like death, back to breaking the law, stealing to get high, back to not having a place to call home, I would lose everything that I have, I would lose my husband, my kids, my family. I would lose myself.

"Come to me, all who are weary and heavy-laden, and I will give you rest."
(Mathew 11:28- NIV)

THE DARKNESS THROUGH ADDICTION

To the 28-year-old reading this,

Who is struggling right now? I was right there with you, and I know what you're going through exactly. It's a shitty place to be and a very dark hole that has no light at the end of it.

You cleaned up once before, but the drug took over your life once again.

You relapsed, and you find yourself in an even deeper dark hole.

You're just going through the motions to stay alive, to just get through the day; you're exhausted, you're lonely, and in your heart, you are missing your family, your parents, your siblings, you're missing your life that it once was.

You have lost everything again, your soul, your life, your family, your belongings, and all you know is the life of addiction.

You've been up for so many days. You keep chasing your next high, and you hope someone welcomes you and lets you stay at their place.

There you are, sitting on the grass or at a bench at the park. Other times you sit on the floor, a bed, or couch – wherever that is that you go get to sleep that night, but you do not care where you get to sleep as long as that pipe is loaded with that next hit.

You make sure of that so you can have that hit when you open your eyes – avoiding having to deal with life. You numb yourself and all your emotions, your feelings.

MY LETTER TO YOU

You feel so lost that you don't even know who you are anymore.

You look at yourself in the mirror and see your face sunk in, your cheekbones sticking out, your hair is a mess because you have not showered for days, you can smell yourself, the smell of death. Your eyes are glossy, and there is no life within them, bags under your eyes, your lips so chapped that you can't even smile because it hurts, and besides, why would you smile? You're not in a good place. Your breath stinks, and your teeth are yellow because you have not brushed your teeth in days. You have been in the same clothes for days on end. You have no life left in you, and you're weak, hungry, and shaking because you can't remember the last time you ate a meal or had something to drink.

You have moments of having drugs in your hand, but you also have times when you have smoked what you were going to sell so you could support your habit. You're selling to get high, a way to support your addiction, and sometimes find yourself smoking what you were supposed to sell to keep your habit, and then you must steal to reload, and the cycle keeps on going.

There are days you wake up, and you have nothing; the anxiety sets in, the withdrawals set in, and you just want life to end.

You are feeling like death. You're tired, and you're exhausted and feeling so hopeless, but yet you know you can't do this anymore, and you want to quit, but you CAN'T. Your body just can't handle it anymore. But you continue to chase the high because that's all your mind and body know what to do. Your body does not know anything different.

You have not showered, brushed your hair or teeth in days, not eaten any food, only the gummy candies you have been stealing from the convenience store.

Those days when you have been up for days on end, can't remember the last time you closed your eyes and got rest. Being so paranoid everywhere you are. You are bouncing around from place to place, being that person who is using people to have a warm shower and hoping that they may feed you or provide some water—or seeking out a bench or nice area in a park where you can have a rest.

You are a complete sketch ball, so paranoid from the sleepless nights and the overuse of the drugs that you think the police are always following you, always looking over your shoulders.

When you want to get higher and start chasing that high and wanting to get higher because you have been at it for a day, you increase your intake and do the chicken on the floor while others around you watch you almost die. Or you see friends around you, while you witness them doing the chicken, you try to comfort them and calm them down as they are having a seizure in your arms, while your heart is racing, you're shaking because you're so scared for this person that may lose their life in your arms.

The thought of being sober is scary, and as an addict, that's the last thing on your mind even if you know you have hit rock bottom and need the change.

Don't beat yourself up. We are only human, and we make mistakes. It's those mistakes that guide us to where we need to be. Mistakes are an essential part of life, so don't fear them. It's okay to make mistakes on your path to recovery as long as you learn from them. So, don't be afraid because you can succeed in your recovery.

Those mistakes are just a bump on the road, and sobriety will not be an easy ride, surround yourself and make sure that you have the support around you to help lift you on those hard days.

Recovery from addiction can be challenging as it takes constant patience and maintenance. Some experience addiction triggers and even relapse. Even if you fall off track and regret your mistakes, it doesn't mean your journey is over. Living an addiction-free life is possible and so WORTH IT!

MY LETTER TO YOU

"Our greatest glory consists not in never falling, but in rising every time we fall" - Oliver Goldsmith

To that 35-year-old reading this,

I was right there with you; who is clean and sober? I know what you are going through exactly.

You're stressed out, your loved one is pissing you off, your kids are getting on your nerves, work is demanding, and you find yourself sitting there thinking and wanting a hit, wanting it to take away that stress you're going through.

You see someone from your past, and you crave, you drive down a road that you got high on, you crave, you drive by a house you got high in you crave, there are so many times that you are craving and that the thought pops into your head.

You are asking yourself, what if I do it once? Nobody will know. Some days are better than others.

It doesn't matter if you are ten days, one year, or 13 years clean you will still crave that drug. You will always have bad days, but it is what you do to get through that bad day. You need to play that tape.

It's not healthy to dwell on the past. Think of your past mistakes as a training ground for the person you've now become. Don't let the regret and guilt from your past behavior burden your present. You must forgive yourself and move on, leave the past behind and focus on the new, sober you.

"Don't let the past steal your present."

THE DARKNESS THROUGH ADDICTION

To that 40-year-old that is reading this,

Who is blaming yourself? I was right there with you, and I know what you are going through.

You lay there in bed, and you can't turn your mind off. You are thinking of your past and everything you did. Everyone that you hurt and betrayed. You are crushed and heartbroken.

You are so ashamed of what you did, the decisions you made, and the loved ones you hurt along the way. You cry quietly, tears run down your face, and you put your face into your pillow so nobody hears you.

You blame yourself for your actions and the mistakes you made along the way! You are casting yourself into a negative light.

Thoughts racing through your mind, "if only I would have …, this wouldn't have happened. It's all my fault."

You begin to second guess yourself. Am I worthy enough? Your confidence is gone, that negative self-talk begins to set in.

Listen! Those are lies you're telling yourself. Shift your mindset; replace those negative thoughts with positive ones!! Put your hand up and admit you need help. Surround yourself with the right people.

Blame is keeping the wounds open, allowing yourself to forgive yourself, and then you can heal from within.

MY LETTER TO YOU

To that the parent, friend, or loved one of an addict reading this,

Who is hurting and praying? My mom is right there with you.

As an addict, I want you to know that there is hope. Please be patient; give that tough love. As hard as it is, give that tough love, do it! That's what my mom did.

Yes, I was not too fond of it, but she saved my life in many ways.

Always believe in your child or loved one. Someone has to believe in them. Your child or loved one is incredible. It's what they are doing or the drug of their choice that makes them do that and become a bad person.

They are unreasonable and sick. Treat them when you can as they had pneumonia; when they are angry at you, remember they are very ill.

You may be able to save them no matter how lost they are; give them space, give them tough love, just let them know they are loved, and always let them know that you are there for them.

It's your love what they remember and can bring them back.

"Courage isn't having the strength not in never falling, but in rising up every time we fall" -
Napoleon Bonaparte

THE DARKNESS THROUGH ADDICTION

Dear reader,

    This journey I faced was what God had planned for me, you see, things happen for a reason, and I believe in my heart that God will use my journey for His plan.

    The experiences that I had to go through, all the times I was nearly dead, He knew it was not my time because His plan was for me to be here today, sharing my journey with you.

    I hope my story helps to encourage you to take the first step to take your life back into your hands.

    For you to overcome this terrible thing called addiction and live your life, being the best version of yourself and living it to your full potential.

Love,

Melissa Corsiatto

XOXOXO

MY LETTER TO YOU

Letter to my Addiction

Now we meet again ... one thing I thought would never happen again. You have caused me nothing but heartache and pain.

I thought I had conquered you, but once again, you have conquered me—what a disappointment.

I believe I have overpowered you, but you had defeated me once again.

I faced my biggest fear, and that fear was you. I thought I was done with you, but I guess you were not done with me.

This time you got your way, and your way almost took my life and nearly destroyed me. You are a piece of shit!!

Because of you, you made me a person I was not and made me make the wrong choices I would not have ever done if you were not present.

My addiction to you caused me to do the worst thing anyone could do, taking away human life. And this also could very well have been me.

You now have made me wake up and made me firmly believe that there may not be a next time.

You made me realize that you can take lives away from innocent people, and it only takes a split second.

I now have to learn to forgive myself for my wrongdoings, which will come in time.

THE DARKNESS THROUGH ADDICTION

But I do have to thank you because of the addiction. I have made wrong decisions which let me be where I am at today, allowed me to my accident, and if it were not for my accident, I would not be clean for 2 ½ months now and changed my life for the better.

This eye-opener has made it easier for me to say NO to you.

I'm not going to let you overpower me again. This is my last chance in life because I know that the next time will be death. If it results in death, then you have overpowered me FOREVER.

I'm going to die overpowering you.

So for our last adventure together, thank you for making me wake up, and now I know I will leave this world overpowering you.

GOODBYE.

Acknowledgments

First to my mom, Debbie, for not giving up on me. Thank you for always being there for me no matter where I was on my journey. Giving me that tough love any addict hates, but that is what saved my life indeed. You are my rock and have always cheered me on. I don't know what I would have done without you. Your support and encouragement during our darkest times and the good times have brought me to where I am today.

To my husband Mic, the love of my life, for teaching me what true love is and showing me how it feels to be loved by someone. You are my love and my best friend, and I don't know what I would have done without you these last 12 years being there by my side. You have been there through the tears, the hard times, and the good times. Your patience with me has been incredible, I know I am not the easiest one to live with, but you continue to show up for me and stand by me every step of the way.

To my boys, I am thankful for your love, light, and heartedness. Having you two in my life has been a true blessing. You are what keeps mommy going. You are my why, and that's why I am driven and determined in everything that I put my heart and soul into because I want to create the best life for you.

To my dad, thank you for the love you gave to me over the years and for never giving up on me.

To my brothers and sisters for the love that I received from each of them, helping me get through treatment and supporting me as I created my new life. For being by my side during the hard times and the good times. To give me the extra hugs and tough love when I needed it most. You all believed in me no matter where I was on my journey.

To my online mentors, thank you! from the bottom of my heart for showing me the path to freedom and choices. You guided me and gave me the roadmap and resources to excel in my business, and not to mention the mentorship I receive from you daily is like no other. You all believe in me, open your arms, and welcome me into your world. Thank you for investing your time in me.

Thanks to Tina Torres, my coach, and friend, for encouraging and pushing me to write this book. I am so blessed that we crossed paths. I would not have written this book if it were not for you. Because of you, I hope to impact the lives of many people. You are an amazing human, friend, and mentor.

To my friends, you know who you are, for being there for me when the tears fell, when the heartache was so strong, and just being there to comfort me and letting me know that I am loved. Thank you for being part of my life, accepting who I am, and always supporting me.

To you reading this book, you are here for a reason; you were guided to me because you needed to hear my story to know that there is hope for you, hope for you to overcome whatever it is that you need to overcome.

Last but not least, to my Father in Heaven for his unconditional love, forgiveness, restored hope, belief, and direction. Thank you for guiding me in such a way I needed to be taught.

About the Author

Melissa Corsiatto is a leader in the online space, an entrepreneur marketing expert, experienced sales coach, and hypnotherapist.

After two years in her Network Marketing business, she retired from her Legal Assistant career to create a lifestyle of choices for her and her family.

Today, Melissa pursues her passion from the comfort of her home. She helps entrepreneurs level up their business to pursue their true passion, enabling her clients to tap into their subconscious minds and work on their limiting beliefs, their mindset letting them reach to the core of what is keeping them stuck.

She is passionate about helping others overcome those obstacles that hold them back in life so that they, too, can create a life of abundance, happiness, and joy.

She lives in Alberta, Canada, where she shares life with her husband Mic and their two boys, Kayden and Kyler.

Made in the USA
Las Vegas, NV
12 February 2022